UZBEKISTAN
in Pictures

Bella Waters

TF CB

Twenty-First Century Books

Contents

Website address: www.lernerbooks.com

Twenty-First Century Books
A division of Lerner Publishing Group
241 First Avenue North
Minneapolis, MN 55401 U.S.A.

web enhanced @ www.vgsbooks.com

Library of Congress Cataloging-in-Publication Data

Waters, Bella.
    Uzbekistan in pictures / by Bella Waters.
        p.   cm. — (Visual geography series)
    Includes bibliographical references and index.
    ISBN-13: 978-0-8225-2673-5 (lib. bdg. : alk. paper)
    ISBN-13: 0-8225-2673-5 (lib. bdg. : alk. paper)
    1. Uzbekistan—Pictorial works—Juvenile literature. I. Title. II. Series: Visual geography series
    (Minneapolis, Minn.)
    DK948.66.W38 2007
    958.7222   2006005463

Manufactured in the United States of America
1 2 3 4 5 6 – BP – 12 11 10 09 08 07

INTRODUCTION

Uzbekistan is a small nation in the center of central Asia. Despite Uzbekistan's small size, its landscape is varied, including vast deserts, fertile river valleys, and snowcapped mountains. The nation is home to approximately 27 million people. These people work in a variety of industries, including oil production, farming, and manufacturing.

As a separate, self-governing nation, Uzbekistan has had a very short history. Its independence dates to 1991, after the breakup of the former Soviet Union. As a culture, however, Uzbekistan is ancient. People have been living in Uzbekistan and the surrounding nations of central Asia for thousands of years. In ancient times, several different empires ruled central Asia. These empires included Persia and Greece.

In the early centuries A.D., central Asia was an important stopping point on the Silk Road. The road was a series of trade routes that linked China, the Middle East, and Europe. Traders along the road

stopped in central Asian cities such as Samarqand, Khiva, and Bukhara, all in modern-day Uzbekistan. The flow of money, goods, and travelers along the road brought prosperity to central Asia.

During the Silk Road era, a series of outsiders invaded central Asia. First the Turks and then the Arabs took over the region. The Arabs brought their religion, Islam, to central Asia. It became the dominant faith of the region. The next conquerors were Mongols, easterners led by the fierce warrior Genghis Khan. In the fourteenth century, a leader named Timur created a powerful empire in central Asia, with Samarqand as its capital. Timur filled the city with grand mosques (Islamic houses of worship) and beautiful artwork.

An ethnic group called the Uzbeks took power in central Asia in the late fifteenth century. Gradually, their power weakened, and Russia, a vast empire to the north, took over all of central Asia. After the Russian Revolution of 1917, central Asia became part of the newly formed Soviet Union. The Soviets divided their nation into fifteen

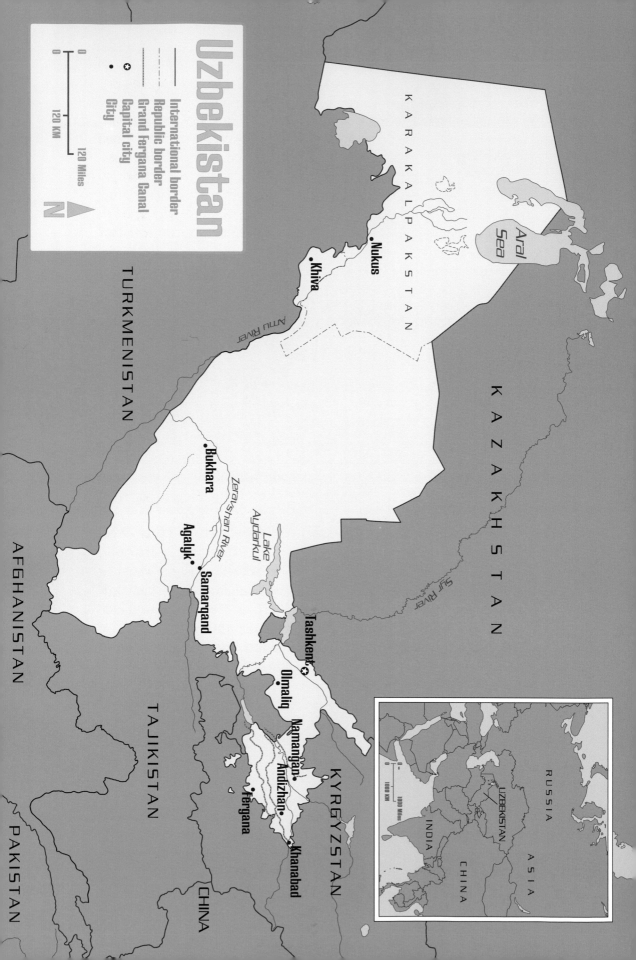

Uzbekistan

K A R A K A L P A K S T A N

Aral Sea

Nukus

Khiva

AMU RIVER

TURKMENISTAN

K A Z A K H S T A N

Bukhara

Zerakshan River

Lake Aydarkul

Agalyk

Samarqand

Tashkent

Syr River

Olmaliq

Namangan

Andizhan

Fergana

Khanabad

KYRGYZSTAN

AFGHANISTAN

TAJIKISTAN

CHINA

PAKISTAN

RUSSIA

A S I A

UZBEKISTAN

INDIA

CHINA

0   1000 Miles
0   1000 KM

republics. One of them was the Uzbek Soviet Socialist Republic—the forerunner of modern-day Uzbekistan.

Soviet rule brought some benefits, such as free health care and education, to the people of Uzbekistan, who collectively came to be called Uzbekistanis. But it also brought many hardships. For instance, the Soviet Union did not give people basic rights and liberties such as freedom of speech, freedom of religion, and the right to vote. Eventually, the Soviet people demanded change. The Soviet Union broke apart in 1991. That same year, Uzbekistan declared itself to be an independent nation.

With independence, many Uzbekistanis were optimistic that freedom, democracy, and prosperity would soon follow. But the switch to independence was rocky for Uzbekistan. Its first president, Islam Karimov, is a former Soviet leader who has refused to make changes to the old Soviet system. He has ruled oppressively, using a secret police force to silence those who oppose him. He has denied rights and religious freedom to his people. His government has kept strict control over Uzbekistan's economy. Elections scheduled for 2007 may lead to a change in the country's leadership.

Meanwhile, in 2001, Uzbekistan entered into an alliance with the United States, which was fighting Islamic extremists in nearby Afghanistan. Meanwhile, the Uzbekistani government clashed with its own Islamic citizens. The nation also faced severe economic problems, such as unemployment, poverty, and high prices.

Uzbekistan remains a poor country. But culturally it is very rich. Uzbekistani craftspeople produce magnificent carpets, metalwork, jewelry, and textiles. Performers carry on centuries-old traditions in song and dance. The ancient cities of Samarqand and Khiva are still filled with awe-inspiring mosques and palaces. The Uzbekistani people are proud of their history and hopeful about their future.

So far, the dream of a free, prosperous, and democratic Uzbekistan has not come true. But many people inside and outside the nation hope to change Uzbekistan for the better. With optimism and hard work, they have a good chance of success.

THE LAND

Located in the heart of central Asia, Uzbekistan is a landlocked nation—a country that does not border any large body of water. The country covers 173,591 square miles (449,601 square kilometers)—an area roughly the size of California. Turkmenistan borders Uzbekistan in the southwest. Kazakhstan lies to the west and north. Kyrgyzstan and Tajikistan are in the east. To the south is Afghanistan. With the exception of Afghanistan, all the nations that surround Uzbekistan are former Soviet republics.

Deserts, Valleys, and Mountains

Uzbekistan has a varied landscape, including dry areas, river valleys, and mountains. The nation's largest region is the Kyzyl Kum (Red Sands) Desert. It stretches across north central Uzbekistan, covering 115,000 square miles (297,850 sq. km) of territory. Few people live in this dry, sandy region. West of the desert sits the Ustyurt Plateau, a dry, stony area that extends west into Kazakhstan.

The Amu River valley, a region of small towns and farms, is southwest of the Kyzyl Kum Desert. East of the desert sit more fertile valleys and plains. These areas hold farms and Uzbekistan's biggest cities. The nation's major valleys are the Zeravshan in east central Uzbekistan, the Chirchik in the northeast, and the Fergana in the east.

Mountains are found on Uzbekistan's far eastern end, surrounding the Fergana Valley. The Tian Mountains spread from Uzbekistan eastward across Kyrgyzstan and western China. The Fan Mountains and the Gissar Mountains straddle Uzbekistan's southeastern border with Tajikistan. The highest point in Uzbekistan is Beshtor Peak, in the Tian Mountains in the nation's far northeast corner. The mountain rises 14,101 feet (4,298 meters) above sea level.

Rivers and Lakes

The Aral Sea is the biggest body of water in Uzbekistan. Despite its name, the Aral Sea is actually a lake—a large body of water surrounded

This photograph of the **Aral Sea** was taken from a space shuttle in 1992.

by land. The sea crosses Uzbekistan's northwestern border with Kazakhstan.

The Aral Sea was once the fourth-largest lake in the world. It measured 25,830 square miles (66,900 sq. km) in area and stretched 250 miles (400 km) from north to south and 175 miles (280 km) from side to side. But in the early 1960s, Soviet engineers began to divert water from the Amu and Syr rivers, which normally flow into the sea. The engineers channeled the water to nearby cotton fields to increase central Asian cotton production.

Without river water to feed it, the Aral Sea began to evaporate, or dry up. By 1987 vast portions of the seabed had been exposed and the sea had split into two sections. By the early years of the twenty-first century, the sea was about 40 percent of its former size and covered only 11,000 square miles (28,490 sq. km).

In addition to the Aral Sea, Uzbekistan is home to Lake Aydarkul, southwest of Tashkent, and a few smaller lakes and marshes.

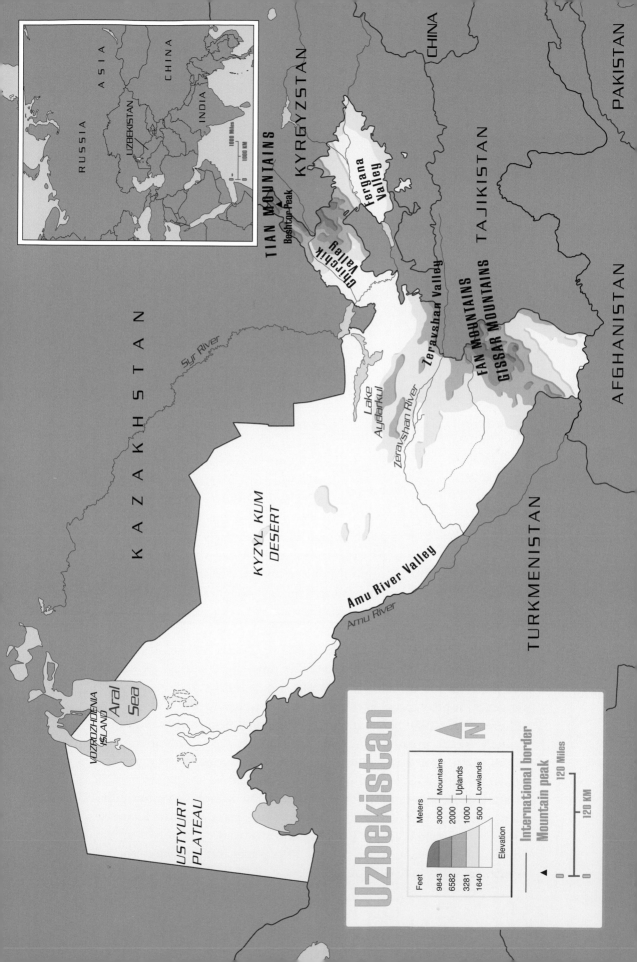

Several rivers, originating in the mountains of surrounding countries, flow through Uzbekistan. The major rivers are the Amu, the Syr, and the Zeravshan. The country also has several canals, or artificial waterways.

Climate

Uzbekistan experiences cold winters and hot summers. The average temperature in January, the coldest month, ranges from 37°F (3°C) in the south to 18°F (–8°C) on the Ustyurt Plateau. But sometimes temperatures go much lower, reaching as low as –35°F (–37°C) on the Ustyurt Plateau in winter. In July, the hottest month, temperatures average 79°F (26°C) in the north and 86°F (30°C) in the south. But in some places, temperatures can soar as high as 113°F (45°C) in summer.

Rainfall varies in Uzbekistan depending on the region. Scant amounts of rain—as little as 4 inches (10 centimeters)—fall annually in the deserts. Mountainous areas receive up to 24 inches (61 cm) of precipitation per year, mostly as snow. The rainiest months are March and April.

In the Kyzyl Kum Desert, the temperature of the sand can rise to 158°F (70°C) on hot summer days. But the desert gets cold too. In winter, temperatures in the Kyzyl Kum can fall to –8°F (–22°C).

Along Uzbekistan's border with Afghanistan, a strong dry wind called the *afghanets* arrives from the southwest. The dusty, dirty gusts—which blow for nearly seventy days in the winter and spring—can clog car parts and other machinery with grit. People who go outdoors have to cover their faces with scarves when the winds are blowing.

Flora and Fauna

With its varied terrain, Uzbekistan is home to a variety of plants and trees. In the east, the mountain slopes hold stands of walnut, pistachio, juniper, pine, apricot, and apple trees. Uzbekistan's plains are home to vast fields of grasses, shrubs, poppies, tulips, and other flowers. Reeds, shrubs, elm trees, and poplar trees grow along the banks of rivers. Tough shrubs that do not need much water grow in the Kyzyl Kum Desert and the Ustyurt Plateau.

Uzbekistan's animal life is also varied. The nation's mountainous areas are home to bears, lynxes, mountain goats, and snow leopards (large brown-spotted cats). Gazelles and Bactrian camels live in the deserts of western Uzbekistan, as do gophers, rats, scorpions, and poisonous snakes. The plains are home to deer and antelope, as well

Hundreds of **poppies** dot a field near the city of Samarqand.

as birds such as ring-necked pheasants, partridges, black grouse, bustards, falcons, and hawks. Wild boars, jackals, and deer live along the riverbanks of Uzbekistan, while carp and other freshwater fish swim in the rivers.

◉ Natural Resources

Uzbekistan is rich in metals, such as gold, copper, lead, silver, tungsten, uranium, and zinc. Rocks and gems—including turquoise, marble, onyx, and garnet—are found in many areas of the country.

Snow leopard

Natural gas is Uzbekistan's major energy resource, with the largest deposits in the Bukhara region. Coal mines lie near the city of Tashkent and in the Gissar Mountain region. Workers extract and process petroleum (fuel oil) in the Fergana Valley, in the Bukhara region, and in southern Uzbekistan. Because it has plentiful deposits of gas, coal, and petroleum, Uzbekistan does not need to import energy from other countries.

About 11 percent of Uzbekistan's land is arable, or suitable for farming, although less than 1 percent of the land is actually planted with crops. The most important crop is cotton. Farmers also grow fruits and vegetables, keep livestock, and raise silkworms. Forests cover just 0.5 percent of Uzbekistan's land.

◉ Environmental Issues

To protect its wildlife, Uzbekistan has created fifteen nature reserves throughout the country. These reserves are off-limits to hunting, logging, building, and other human activities. However, loggers sometimes illegally cut down trees in the reserves. Hunters illegally kill wild animals such as sheep, bears, antelope, and deer. The government has weak environmental laws and is unable to stop such activity. As a result, many plant and animal species have greatly declined in numbers.

Farming and industry also contribute to environmental destruction. Herders have allowed livestock to overgraze on the plains. The animals eat vast amounts of grassland, leaving the soil dry and lifeless. This process causes desertification—the transformation of fertile land into desert. Cotton growers use large amounts of pesticides and fertilizers on their crops. These dangerous chemicals have filtered into the nation's soil, water, and food supply.

During the Soviet era, the government used Vozrozhdenia Island in the Aral Sea to test biological and chemical weapons. The government also stored nuclear waste in Kyrgyzstan near the Uzbekistani border. But safety standards were loose, and dangerous biological, chemical, and nuclear substances have polluted the surrounding air and water. Waste from mining and industry has also polluted Uzbekistan's air, lakes, and rivers. Such pollution leads to cancer, asthma, and other illnesses in people.

One of the worst environmental problems facing Uzbekistan is the

A USEFUL ANIMAL

In earlier centuries, Uzbekistanis and other central Asians often traveled on camelback. In modern times, few people travel this way. But Uzbekistanis still raise camels for their milk and meat. People make clothing and blankets out of camel hair and make shoes and bags from camel hide. The camels that live in Uzbekistan are Bactrian camels, which have long thick hair and two humps.

destruction of the Aral Sea. The sea once had clean water, sandy beaches, and great amounts of fish. The fish supported a large fishing industry. But then, with the diversion of river water to irrigate cotton fields, the sea started to dry up. As the sea shrunk, most of its fish died. Fishers could no longer make a living from the sea. Making matters worse, pesticides and fertilizers from surrounding agriculture fields polluted the remaining water.

With so much less water in the sea, the surrounding air grew drier. Less rain fell. Winds whipped up vast storms of salt, sand, and dust from the exposed seafloor, often sickening people who lived nearby. The sea's polluted water also made people sick. Animals and plants were no longer able to live in the water or around the shore.

In the late 1980s, leaders in Uzbekistan and Kazakhstan realized that the destruction of the sea had to stop. Since then the nations of central Asia have started to increase the flow of water into the sea. These efforts should help clean up pollution, treat the public health problems caused by the sea's destruction, and save some of the plant and animal life around the sea. International organizations such as the World Bank and the United Nations have also gotten involved in the fight to restore the Aral Sea.

This abandoned ship once sat on the edge of the Aral Sea. Beached ships are a common sight along the shores of the sea, which has receded more than 62 miles (100 km) since the diversion of the rivers that feed it began in 1964.

▶ Cities

Uzbekistan's big cities—Tashkent, Samarqand, Bukhara, and others—are steeped in history. Many sit on the former Silk Road, the famous trade route of earlier centuries. They once hosted travelers from far-off lands to the east and west. Of Uzbekistan's 27 million people, roughly 37 percent live in cities.

TASHKENT (population 2.3 million), the capital of Uzbekistan, is the biggest and most important city in central Asia. Historians think the first settlement at Tashkent was Ming-Uruk, an ancient town dating to the first or second century B.C. The town became a major stop for traders on the Silk Road. It got the name Tashkent, or City of Stone, in the eleventh century A.D. (Historians think the name comes from inhabitants being as strong as stone in defending their city.)

Over the centuries, as various outside empires ruled central Asia, Tashkent remained an important city. It became the capital of the Uzbek Soviet Socialist Republic in 1930. Also during the Soviet era,

Tashkent became a major industrial center. In 1966 a powerful earthquake hit Tashkent. The quake destroyed many of the city's historic structures and left 300,000 people homeless. After the city was rebuilt, it had a more modern appearance, with factories, government offices, concrete apartment buildings, and a subway system.

Although it has a modern feel, many historic sites remain in Tashkent. Examples include Old Town, with narrow streets and centuries-old mosques and madrassas (Islamic religious schools). The city is ethnically diverse. In addition to Uzbeks, many Russians, Tatars, and other ethnic groups live there.

SAMARQAND (population 405,000), in the Zeravshan Valley, is one of the oldest settlements in central Asia. People first lived there in the fifth century B.C. The city has witnessed many invaders, including the Macedonian general Alexander the Great in ancient times and the Mongol warrior Genghis Khan, who completely destroyed the city in 1220. A later Mongol commander, Timur, rebuilt Samarqand into a grand city. When Uzbekistan became the Uzbek Soviet Socialist Republic, Samarqand was its first capital.

Modern Samarqand is a mixture of old and new. Many impressive buildings of Timur's day remain. But broad paved streets, modern factories and office buildings, and Soviet-era apartment houses are found here as well.

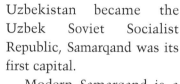

Samarqand's city center features many old Islamic buildings standing among more modern buildings.

EARTHQUAKE PRONE

Earthquakes occur when the earth's rocky outer shell breaks or shifts. Some areas are more prone to earthquakes than others. Uzbekistan's Fergana Valley is an earthquake-prone region, and several earthquakes have hit the area in recent history. The 1902 Andizhan quake and the 1966 Tashkent quake are two examples.

ANDIZHAN (population 350,000) is Uzbekistan's easternmost big city, located near the Kyrgyzstan border. The city dates to the ninth century A.D. and was a major stop on the Silk Road. A big earthquake hit Andizhan in 1902 and killed many of its residents. In modern times, Andizhan is an industrial city. It has a large car factory run by Daewoo, a South Korean–based company. Many oil wells and oil refineries are near the city.

BUKHARA (population 255,000) is an economic hub in the Zeravshan Valley. Its history dates to the ninth century A.D. Early Bukhara was an Islamic center, with mosques, madrassas, and many religious leaders. It was also a Silk Road town and a center of art, music, and learning. In modern times, Bukhara is still a religious center. It is also home to food-processing, handicraft, and other industries.

A view of Bukhara from the Kalan Minaret (tower), the most prominent landmark in the city. The tower has been used as a watchtower in times of war, and local tradition holds that criminals sentenced to death were thrown from the top, earning the tower the nickname Tower of Death.

Visit www.vgsbooks.com for links to websites with additional information about the many things to see and do in Uzbekistan's cities, as well as links to websites about Uzbekistan's weather, natural resources, plants and animals, and more.

KHIVA (population 50,000) has been inhabited since ancient times, although its precise history is unknown. In the early centuries A.D., it was a stopping point on the Silk Road. In the sixteenth century, it was the capital of the Khiva khanate (a small kingdom). Khiva fell to Russian invaders in 1873. In the 1970s and 1980s, Soviet city planners restored many of Khiva's old mosques, tombs, palaces, madrassas, and city walls. In modern times, the city is a magnet for tourists to Uzbekistan.

HISTORY AND GOVERNMENT

Archaeological evidence, such as pottery, weapons, and tools, shows that humans have lived in central Asia since prehistoric times. The first inhabitants that historians can identify by name are the Indo-Iranians. They were nomads—people without permanent dwellings. About five thousand years ago, the Indo-Iranians migrated from their homeland in southern Russia, through central Asia and then on to new lands in India and in Iran (then called Persia). By about 2000 B.C., some people in central Asia had settled into permanent farms and villages. The farmers grew crops such as wheat, barley, and millet. They also raised sheep, cattle, and horses.

Starting around 1000 B.C., a great empire developed in Persia, southwest of central Asia in modern-day Iran. The Persian Empire reached its peak under Cyrus the Great. In the 500s B.C., Cyrus greatly expanded his empire. His armies captured Middle Eastern lands to the west and central Asian lands to the east. The Persians divided their empire into provinces. The lands of modern-day

Uzbekistan were split among the Persian provinces of Chorasmia, Bactria, and Sogdiana.

In 334 B.C., Alexander the Great, a Macedonian whose kingdom was based in Greece, invaded the Persian Empire. In a campaign lasting several years, Alexander's armies traveled east, conquering as they went. After conquering the Persian provinces of central Asia, Alexander married a Bactrian princess.

Alexander returned west in 325 B.C., but he did not have long to rule his vast new kingdom. He sickened and died in 323 B.C. Afterward, his generals divided his empire among themselves. A general named Seleucus took charge of Persian lands in central Asia. Seleucus and his successors ruled central Asia for several hundred years.

In the first century A.D., the Kushan people came to power in central Asia. The Kushan were based in northern Afghanistan, but their ancestors had come from western China. Kushan kings practiced the Asian religion of Buddhism and introduced this religion to central Asia.

⊙ The Silk Road Era

Starting in this era, traders traveled between China and Europe along a series of routes called the Silk Road (so named because silk was a prized Chinese trade item). At about the halfway point, the routes passed through central Asia. For centuries, central Asian

Camel caravans traveled the Silk Road between China and the Mediterranean Sea for more than fifteen hundred years. People came to Uzbekistan along the Silk Road for the powerful horses of the Fergana Valley.

townspeople provided food, water, housing, fresh horses and camels, and banking services to travelers along the road. The constant flow of goods, money, and travelers brought prosperity to central Asia. It also brought great cultural exchange, since travelers of diverse nations, religions, and languages mingled along the road.

This peaceful and prosperous existence was shattered by a Turkish invasion of central Asia in the sixth century A.D. The Turks, who came from the north, seized valuable trade routes and took control of central Asian cities.

Another invasion occurred in the eighth century, when Arab warriors arrived from the Middle East. The Arabs tried to impose their religion, Islam, on the local people. The locals practiced their own ancient religions and at first resisted Islamic teachings. But gradually, many people in central Asia converted to the Islamic faith.

The vast Arab Empire, which stretched from North Africa to India, was too big to govern without the help of local leaders. In the ninth century, Saman-khoda, a Persian noble who worked for the Arabs, took control in central Asia. He and his successors—called the Samanid dynasty—ruled central Asia for more than one hundred years.

Samanid power declined at the end of the tenth century. Afterward, new independent kingdoms emerged in central Asia, including the Ghaznavid state in the south and the Khorezm state in the west. By the late twelfth century, Khorezm had become the most powerful kingdom in central Asia.

New Conquerors

Khorezm's power was short lived. In the early thirteenth century, a huge army of Mongol warriors arrived in central Asia from the east. Guided by their leader, Genghis Khan (a title meaning "supreme

THE SILK ROAD

The Silk Road flourished from about 100 B.C. to A.D. 1500. Traders carried silk, porcelain, paper, jade, tea, spices, and perfumes from China, westward through central Asia, and on to the Middle East and Asia Minor (modern Turkey). The traders traveled in large groups called caravans. They crossed vast deserts and high mountains. They used camels and other animals to carry heavy loads. When the traders reached ports on the Black and Mediterranean seas, they loaded their goods onto boats for shipment to Europe. Then the traders loaded up with goods from Europe, Africa, and the Middle East, including gold, silver, furs, honey, ivory, and glass. They carried these items back to China.

This woodcut shows **Genghis Khan leading his Mongol warriors.** The Mongol Empire was the largest land empire in history.

prince"), the Mongols attacked in 1220. Mongol warriors killed people by the thousands and destroyed cities and farms.

Mongol leaders controlled much of Asia throughout the thirteenth and fourteenth centuries. In central Asia, a Mongol warrior named Timur (also known as Tamerlane) came to power in the late fourteenth century. A descendant of Genghis Khan, Timur had been born near Samarqand. Starting in the 1370s, his armies conquered territory from the Black Sea in the west to India in the east, creating the Timurid Empire. Timur made Samarqand the capital of his empire.

Timur was a savage conqueror and a brutal ruler, but he had an artistic side. He invited writers, architects, craftspeople, and musicians from conquered territories to Samarqand. He directed the artists to create jewelry, glasswork, weavings, and paintings.

Timur (or Tamerlane)

Timur's architects built libraries, gardens, fountains, and bazaars. The musicians composed and performed songs and dances. Writers created poetry. Timur was also a devout Muslim (follower of Islam), and he oversaw the building of glittering mosques in Samarqand.

After Timur's death in 1405, Mongol power declined, enabling other groups to take control in central Asia. In the late fifteenth and early sixteenth centuries, a group called the Uzbeks conquered the remains of the Timurid Empire. By the time the Uzbeks took power, the Silk Road had decreased in importance. Instead of traveling by land, European and Asian merchants began to travel the globe in boats, along newly discovered sea routes. The decline in overland trade hurt central Asia's economy.

Weakened by the loss of trade, Uzbek territory broke into khanates. These states were each headed by a khan, or prince. The khanates of Bukhara and Khiva emerged in the sixteenth century, and the khanate of Quqon formed in the eighteenth century. Frequent wars among the khanates hurt their ability to fend off attacks by foreign powers.

○ **Russian Rule**

By the eighteenth century, Russia was a growing power in Europe and Asia. Based in the city of Saint Petersburg, Russian leaders set about increasing their strength and territory. They began to invade surrounding lands. In the 1850s, Russia took territory from the Kazakhs in central Asia, from the Ottoman Turks farther west, and from the Chinese farther east. Then Russia set its sights on the rest of central Asia. In the 1860s and 1870s, Russian forces seized Quqon, Bukhara, and finally Khiva. By the 1880s, Russia controlled central Asia south to the present-day Afghanistan border.

Russia was quick to use the new territory it had gained in central Asia. On the lands of modern-day Uzbekistan, the Russians set up cotton plantations (large farms) and factories that processed raw cotton and other agricultural products. To transport the products, the Russians built railway lines that connected central Asia's major cities to cities in Russia.

The Russians also awarded central Asian lands to millions of settlers from Russia. The central Asians and the Russian newcomers lived very different lives. The central Asians practiced Islam and lived as their ancestors had done for generations—running small farms and raising livestock. Some of them were nomadic—traveling from place to place in search of fresh grazing land for their animals. The Russians, on the other hand, practiced Orthodox Christianity. They were used to a more urban lifestyle, with then-modern conveniences such as telegraph lines, paved streets, and theaters.

Russia ruled over its expanding empire from **Saint Petersburg,** where the royals resided in fabulous palaces such as Catherine Palace, above.

Central Asian natives resented both the newcomers and their new rulers in Saint Petersburg. Occasionally, local people rebelled against Russian authorities. For instance, natives of Andizhan rose up against Russian rule in 1897 and 1898. Russian soldiers put down this uprising as well as several others around the same time.

Resentment against the Russians grew even greater when Russia entered World War I (1914–1918). The Russian government demanded that its central Asian provinces provide vast amounts of cotton, food, cattle, and workers for the war effort. When the local people resisted the taking of their resources, the Russians responded by massacring citizens and burning villages.

The Soviet Takeover

The Russian people had been dissatisfied with their czar, or emperor, for many years. Many Russians demanded a new form of government for their nation. In 1917 political activists called Bolsheviks led a revolution in Russia. The revolutionaries toppled the czar and set up a Communist government.

Citizens of Samarqand protest against the Communist takeover in 1917.

Under the Communist system, the government completely controlled the nation's economy, business, and labor force. Private property was abolished. A small group of Communist Party leaders ran the government from a new capital in Moscow, southwest of Saint Petersburg. The Communist Party was the only political party allowed to operate.

Many people in central Asia and other Russian-controlled territories did not want to live under Communist rule. Right after the Bolshevik takeover, citizens formed an army to fight Communist forces. But over the course of several years, the Communists prevailed.

In 1922 Communist Party leaders gave their nation a new name: the Union of Soviet Socialist Republics (USSR, also called the Soviet Union). Over the next eighteen years, the Soviet government divided the nation into fifteen republics. In central Asia, these republics were Uzbekistan, Kazakhstan, Turkmenistan, Kirghiz, and Tajikistan.

◉ Life under the Soviets

The new Soviet Union was the world's largest country. The fifteen Soviet republics were home to more than one hundred ethnic groups, speaking dozens of different languages. In central Asia, people spoke Kazakh, Kyrgyz, Tajik, Turkmen, or Uzbek, depending on where they lived. Most people in Uzbekistan spoke Uzbek. The central Asians wrote their languages using the Arabic alphabet.

Of the fifteen Soviet republics, Russia was the biggest by far. Moscow, the Soviet capital, was in Russia, and Russians held the most important positions in the Soviet government. To increase national unity and loyalty, the government tried to Russify the people

Two young Uzbekistani women study botany at a **collective farm** created by the Soviet government.

of central Asia and other non-Russian republics—that is, to make them behave more like Russians. As part of this effort, the government made Russian the official language of the whole Soviet Union. In central Asia, the Soviet government replaced the Arabic alphabet first with the Latin alphabet (also used to write English) and then with the Cyrillic alphabet, used to write Russian.

Economically, the government had a master plan for the nation. The government seized land from farmers and created large collective, or state-owned, farms. Farmers who had formerly worked their own land became state employees on collective farms. Nomadic peoples were forced to give up their traveling lifestyle and settle down on collective farms. In Uzbekistan the government devoted vast amounts of land to growing cotton, used to make clothing.

People who resisted the Soviet government in any way faced severe punishment. The government often imprisoned and even killed those who spoke out against collectivization or other government programs. The worst repression occurred in the 1930s, after Joseph Stalin took control of the Soviet government. Stalin ordered the imprisonment or execution of millions of Soviet citizens, including tens of thousands of central Asians.

In 1939 the Soviet Union entered World War II (1939–1945), at first on the German side and later on the Allied side. During the conflict, Joseph Stalin grew suspicious of minority groups in the Soviet Union. Fearing that minority citizens might assist the enemy, Stalin sent many of them from their homes on the edges of the Soviet Union to live in remote central Asia. The ethnic groups included Koreans, Armenians, Georgians, Tatars, and Chechens. This influx of newcomers created a greater ethnic mix in Uzbekistan and other central Asian republics.

In the decades following World War II (which ended in victory for the Soviet Union and the Allies), the Soviet government set up heavy industries, such as machine assembly and textile manufacturing, in Uzbekistan. Cotton production continued to be a major industry. The government also created engineering projects to channel the waters of the Amu and Syr rivers to vast cotton fields. This process caused a great ecological disaster: the drying up of the Aral Sea.

Although the Soviet government was harsh and repressive, it did bring many improvements to Uzbekistan and other central Asian nations. For

These men watch the Syr River enter the **Fergana Canal,** which they helped build. The canal diverts water from the river to irrigate nearby cotton fields.

instance, the government provided jobs, health care, and education to all its citizens. In central Asia, literacy rates (the number of people who could read and write) climbed to 97 percent under the Soviet system. Women were given equal status with men in employment and education.

Independence

But the Soviet Union did not give people the right to vote, freedom of speech, freedom of religion, and other liberties that people enjoy in democratic countries. After nearly seventy years of heavy-handed Soviet rule, Soviet people began to demand change.

In the 1980s, the Soviet leader Mikhail Gorbachev introduced the policy of glasnost, which means "openness" in the Russian language. This policy gave the Soviet people more freedom to express their political opinions. Throughout the Soviet Union, people began to form new political groups. In Uzbekistan, writers and scholars created Birlik (Unity), a movement dedicated to improving Uzbekistani society and the environment.

Back in Moscow, some Soviet leaders opposed glasnost. They felt it threatened their power and authority. In August 1991, a group of Communist leaders tried to overthrow Mikhail Gorbachev. In Moscow and other cities, people protested against the takeover, which quickly failed. By then the central Soviet government had grown weak. Within days of the failed takeover, republics throughout the Soviet Union began declaring their independence. Following the lead of larger republics, Uzbekistan proclaimed self-rule in September 1991.

The Soviet Union had fallen apart. The fifteen Soviet republics set up new governments and held elections. In Uzbekistan, voters chose Islam Karimov, former head of the Communist Party of Uzbekistan, as the first president of a self-governing Uzbekistan. But the election that brought Karimov to the presidency was hardly democratic. Karimov's party harassed and silenced members of two popular opposing parties, Erk (an offshoot of Birlik) and the Islamic Renaissance Party. Critics say that Karimov's group also tampered with votes at the ballot box. After the elections, Karimov and other former Communist Party leaders still ruled Uzbekistan, only under a different party name.

NEW NAMES

Uzbekistan is trying to rid itself of reminders of the Soviet Union. In the city of Fergana, for instance, Communist Street has been renamed Samarqand Street. Karl Marx Street was originally named for a nineteenth-century philosopher whose ideas formed the basis for Communism. The street's new name is Fergana Street.

Visit www.vgsbooks.com for links to websites with additional information about the history of Uzbekistan, including the rise and fall of the Soviet Union, Uzbekistani independence, and President Karimov.

Off to a Bad Start

In 1992 Uzbekistan joined the United Nations, an international organization that works for world peace and human rights. Uzbekistan also created a constitution in 1992. The constitution stated that Uzbekistan was a democratic nation, with freedom of speech and freedom of religion.

The reality was quite different from the constitution, however. In actuality, Islam Karimov ruled as a dictator. He passed laws that increased his power and changed the constitution to extend his term. He set up a strong secret police force and took control of the legislative (lawmaking) and judicial branches of government. He used his secret police to arrest opponents and to shut down newspapers that

President Islam Karimov is a controversial ruler. Though he has allies in the United States and Russia, he is also a harsh ruler who denies people human rights.

UZBEKISTANI INJUSTICE

Corruption and abuse mar Uzbekistan's system of justice. Police officers often arrest people on vague charges, such as "conspiracy to commit terrorism" or "anti-constitutional activity." The police routinely hold suspects for months, without giving them trials or contact with lawyers. Police officers often use beatings and torture to get people to confess to crimes, whether they committed them or not. Trials are often one sided in favor of the government. Prison conditions are harsh. Prisoners don't get adequate food, medicine, or toilet facilities. Relatives who want their family members to receive decent treatment in prison must bribe prison guards.

criticized him. Many of his critics fled to Russia, Turkey, or countries in Europe.

Most ordinary citizens were afraid to speak out against the government. But one group—radical Muslims—dared to challenge Karimov's power. The Islamic Movement of Uzbekistan and the Islamic Party of Liberation wanted to create an Islamic government in Uzbekistan. In the mid-1990s, these groups committed shootings, bombings, and other terrorist acts directed against the government. To suppress the movement, President Karimov imposed strict controls on Islamic worship. His police force arrested, imprisoned, and tortured Islamic citizens who refused to follow the rules. The police also punished the relatives of Islamic activists.

In late 1999 and early 2000, Uzbekistanis again went to the polls to vote for government leaders. Islam Karimov ran for reelection and won a landslide victory. But foreign observers charged that the elections had not been free or fair. They noted that parties opposed to the Karimov government were barred from participation. Voters were not allowed to attend political meetings, and the government controlled the balloting and counted the votes.

◉ War Abroad and at Home

Many nations, including the United States, condemned Karimov's repressive government. But in the first years of the twenty-first century, the U.S. government saw that Uzbekistan could be a useful ally in its global war on terror. As part of this war, the United States attacked a corrupt government in Afghanistan that had ties to terrorist groups. The campaign in Afghanistan began in October 2001.

Uzbekistan sits on Afghanistan's northern border. For easy access to Afghanistan, the United States wanted to set up a military base in Uzbekistan. Uzbekistan agreed, and the two governments became allies in the war on terror. In return for its help, the United States gave Uzbekistan millions of dollars in financial aid.

But even with U.S. assistance, Uzbekistan faced severe troubles. About 80 percent of its people lived in poverty. Many were unemployed. Tight government control kept the economy from growing strong. The government continued its repressive tactics, especially against devout Muslims.

In May 2005, in the city of Andizhan, Uzbekistani soldiers fired on a crowd that had gathered to protest government repression, poverty, and unemployment, and the jailing of twenty-three local Islamic businessmen. International human rights groups say the soldiers killed more than seven hundred people, including women and children. The Uzbekistani government says that far fewer people were killed and that the demonstrators were Islamic terrorists.

Troops in armored vehicles kept guard in Andizhan following the May 2005 shootings. For a brief time, no one was allowed to enter or leave the city. Soldiers and Islamic militants frequently clash in the region.

The killing of civilians angered many people in the United States. The U.S. government threatened to withhold aid from Uzbekistan if it did not improve its human rights record. The United States also requested an international investigation of the events in Andizhan. The European Union, an alliance of European nations, also condemned the violence.

But Uzbekistani leaders admitted no wrongdoing. Rather than comply with U.S. demands, Uzbekistan told the United States to withdraw its soldiers from Uzbekistan by early 2006. (The troops left in November 2005.) U.S.-Uzbekistani cooperation was over for the moment. But the United States still hoped to keep Uzbekistan as an ally in the war on terror.

The Uzbekistani people, meanwhile, remain mired in poverty, in despair, and in fear of government police. President Karimov's term in office is due to end in 2007. Many people in Uzbekistan hope that a change in leadership will bring political and economic improvements to their nation.

REPRESSION AND RADICALISM

International observers condemn President Karimov's repressive government for many reasons. First and foremost, the repression is unjust. It denies people basic rights and freedoms. Second, many political experts worry that Karimov's harsh repression will drive more and more Uzbekistanis to join the radical Islamic movement, the only organized and active political movement in Uzbekistan. This trend worries many people in the United States and other nations who fear the growing power of radical Islam.

◉ Government

According to the Uzbekistani constitution, adopted in 1992, Uzbekistan is a republic—a nation with an elected government. All citizens eighteen years and older are eligible to vote.

Voters elect a president for a seven-year term, with a two-term limit. The president appoints a prime minister and deputy ministers, who handle the day-to-day business of running the government.

The Uzbekistani legislature consists of an upper house, or Senate, with 100 members, and a lower house, or Legislative Chamber, with 120 members. The president appoints 16 Senate members, and regional governing councils elect the other 84 Senate members. Citizens elect members of the Legislative Chamber. All members of the legislature serve five-year terms.

Uzbekistan's judicial system consists of a Supreme Court, local courts, and military courts. The president has the power to appoint and remove judges.

For purposes of regional government, Uzbekistan is divided into twelve provinces, one autonomous (self-governing) republic (Karakalpakstan), and one city (Tashkent). The president appoints a chief executive to oversee each region. Voters in each region also elect a governing council that handles local government issues. Compared to the national government, Uzbekistan's regional governments are very weak.

KARAKALPAKSTAN

Karakalpakstan, in western Uzbekistan, was an autonomous region within Uzbekistan during Soviet days. After Uzbekistan gained independence in 1991, Karakalpakstan retained its autonomous status. In reality, however, the central Uzbekistani government maintains tight control in Karakalpakstan as it does in all other regions. The region takes its name from the Karakalpak ethnic group, which makes up about one-third of the population there. The name *Karakalpak* means "Black Hat People." Presumably, the Karakalpaks once were famous for wearing black hats, although historians can't confirm this.

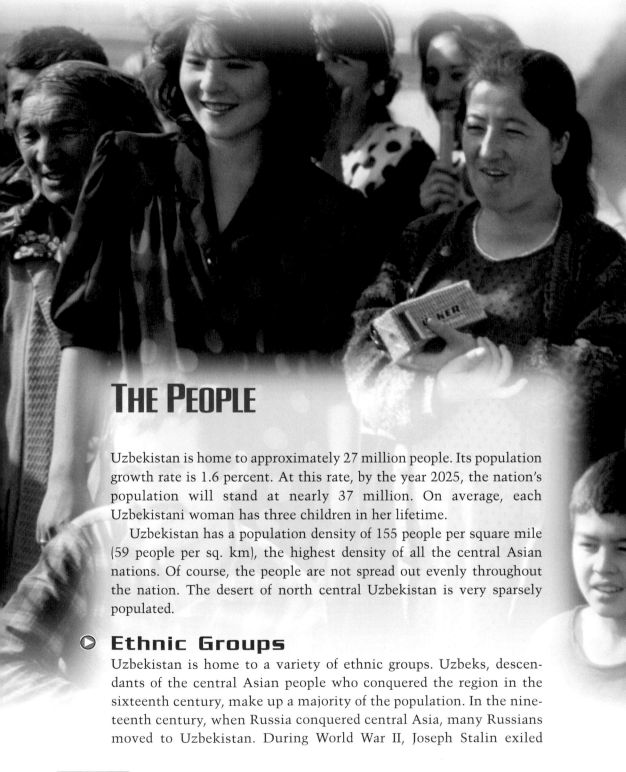

THE PEOPLE

Uzbekistan is home to approximately 27 million people. Its population growth rate is 1.6 percent. At this rate, by the year 2025, the nation's population will stand at nearly 37 million. On average, each Uzbekistani woman has three children in her lifetime.

Uzbekistan has a population density of 155 people per square mile (59 people per sq. km), the highest density of all the central Asian nations. Of course, the people are not spread out evenly throughout the nation. The desert of north central Uzbekistan is very sparsely populated.

Ethnic Groups

Uzbekistan is home to a variety of ethnic groups. Uzbeks, descendants of the central Asian people who conquered the region in the sixteenth century, make up a majority of the population. In the nineteenth century, when Russia conquered central Asia, many Russians moved to Uzbekistan. During World War II, Joseph Stalin exiled

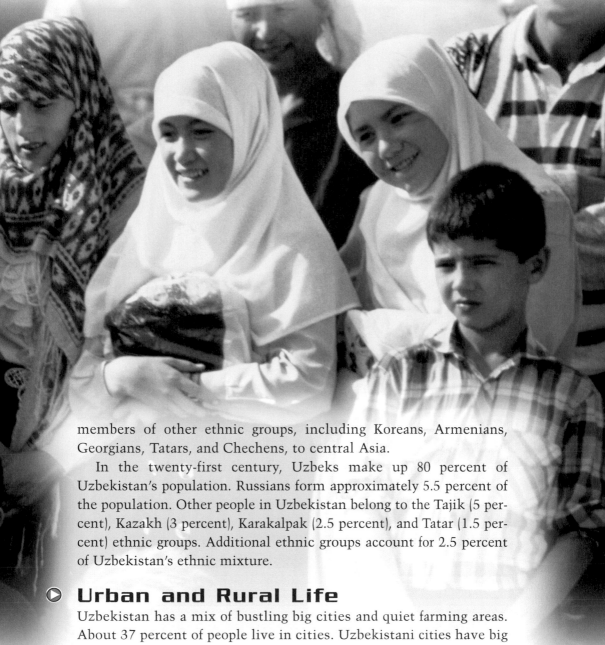

members of other ethnic groups, including Koreans, Armenians, Georgians, Tatars, and Chechens, to central Asia.

In the twenty-first century, Uzbeks make up 80 percent of Uzbekistan's population. Russians form approximately 5.5 percent of the population. Other people in Uzbekistan belong to the Tajik (5 percent), Kazakh (3 percent), Karakalpak (2.5 percent), and Tatar (1.5 percent) ethnic groups. Additional ethnic groups account for 2.5 percent of Uzbekistan's ethnic mixture.

▶ Urban and Rural Life

Uzbekistan has a mix of bustling big cities and quiet farming areas. About 37 percent of people live in cities. Uzbekistani cities have big public plazas, broad boulevards, vast open-air markets, and large statues of Timur and other heroes. Cities are a mix of old and new, with blocks of modern-style apartment buildings as well as historic sections dating to the Middle Ages (A.D. 500 to 1500) and even earlier.

As in big cities everywhere, buses, taxis, and private cars rush through the streets. Tashkent has a clean and efficient subway system. Urban dwellers in Uzbekistan work in stores, factories, and office buildings. To relax and socialize, they go to restaurants, cafes, teahouses, and nightclubs.

The *mahalla*, or neighborhood, is the center of urban life. A mahalla might encompass a large apartment building or a neighborhood of single-family homes. The typical mahalla has about two thousand residents. Within each mahalla, families help one another with projects such as home improvement, street cleaning, or assistance for the elderly. Residents in each mahalla elect a chairperson and a group of advisers. These officials act as a local governing council, settling disputes and making decisions on local issues.

Most big cities are found in the east, especially in the densely populated Fergana Valley. Farther west, there are fewer and fewer people. Karakalpakstan in the west has the fewest towns and farms. The land around the Aral Sea is particularly bleak. Because the sea has dried up, the land is dusty and lifeless. People who used to make a living by fishing in the sea have packed up and left. Boats once docked in deep water lie stranded on dry land.

Some rural dwellers live in small towns. They work as shopkeepers, miners, or mechanics, depending on the local economy. But most rural dwellers—about 60 percent— make their living by farming. The typical Uzbekistani farm is owned and run by a single family. Many farmers harvest cotton, while others grow grain or fruit. Some farmers raise sheep, cattle,

OLD-STYLE HOMES

In earlier centuries, Uzbekistanis lived in houses made of sun-dried clay bricks. The typical house was built around a central courtyard, filled with shady trees. Family members used the courtyard for storage, cooking, and socializing. People heated their homes using fire pits or fireplaces. They gathered water from rivers or wells. Some nomadic people, especially in Karakalpakstan, lived in yurts—circular tents made of animal skins, felt, and a wooden frame.

During the Soviet era, the government built many concrete apartment buildings in Uzbekistani cities and towns. But many people continued to live in old courtyard houses. In modern times, Uzbekistani houses are a mix of old and new. Some people live in old clay brick homes, while others live in more modern buildings.

Uzbekistani farmers pose outside a **yurt** near Khiva. Uzbekistanis sometimes use yurts as temporary shelters.

goats, and other livestock. Most farms in Uzbekistan have irrigation systems.

Rural life in Uzbekistan has a slower pace than urban life. But in many ways, life is the same everywhere. In both urban and rural areas, people value family ties. Many Uzbekistanis live in multigenerational households, with children, parents, and grandparents sharing the same home. Hospitality is extremely important. Guests bring candy and gifts for their hosts. Hosts ply their guests with food and tea. Uzbekistanis everywhere maintain age-old rituals and ceremonies regarding birth, death, marriage, and other important events.

◉ Education

The Uzbekistani government provides eleven years of public schooling for all children. Children begin primary school at the age of seven. At the age of sixteen, they enter secondary school, or high school. When Uzbekistan was part of the Soviet Union, students learned their lessons in Russian. With independence, most schools switched the language of instruction to Uzbek. Some Uzbekistani students learn English, French, and Arabic, as well as math, history, science, and other academic subjects.

In big cities in Uzbekistan, most school-age children attend school regularly. However, some children drop out of school and take jobs to help support their families. Many children in rural areas work on farms—for part or all of the year—instead of attending school. Some teenagers attend vocational schools, which offer job training instead of academic courses. Some Uzbekistani parents would like to send their children to private Islamic schools instead of public schools. However, the Uzbekistani government has shut down many Islamic schools as part of its fight against Islamic extremism.

Under the Soviet system, education was a high priority, and the government spent large amounts of money on schools. Since the

UZBEKISTANI STYLE

The traditional Uzbekistani outfit consists of a long multicolored overcoat with a bright colored sash for men. Men also wear fur hats or dark skullcaps with white embroidery. Women wear brightly colored, velvet dresses, sometimes with trousers beneath. They often wear head scarves and tie up their hair in braids. Traditional dress is common in the countryside and small towns. In big cities, some people wear Western-style clothing— similar to that seen in Europe and the United States. For instance, some men wear slacks, jackets, and button-down shirts. Some women wear high heels, short skirts, and other Western fashions.

This Uzbekistani wears the **traditional dress** of his ancestors.

Pupils work at their desks in a school in Agalyk, Uzbekistan. Some poor children in Uzbekistan are not able to attend school.

fall of the Soviet Union, schools in Uzbekistan have not been as well funded. Many schools do not have enough supplies. School buildings often go without needed repairs, and teachers' pay is low. Nevertheless, Uzbekistani children manage to learn their lessons. The nation has a high literacy rate. In 2004 the Uzbekistani government reported an adult literacy rate of 99 percent.

When Uzbekistanis greet one another, they make a slight bow and place a hand on the heart. They also gently touch or grasp one another's hand.

Uzbekistan has several colleges and universities. The National University of Uzbekistan (formerly the University of Tashkent) and Samarqand State University offer courses in physics, math, history, foreign languages, writing, and other areas of study. Other colleges train students in farming, medicine, teaching, engineering, and other professions.

◉ Health Care

Under the Soviet system, people in Uzbekistan received free health care. After Uzbekistan became independent, private health insurance companies, hospitals, clinics, and doctors' offices opened in many places. The government also still provided some health services to citizens.

Unfortunately for patients, the quality of medical care after independence was not as high as that provided under Soviet rule. Many skilled doctors and nurses, especially ethnic Russians, left Uzbekistan in the 1990s, leaving the nation short on health-care staff.

In the early years of the twenty-first century, Uzbekistan's health care is substandard. In some places in the country, common medicines and trained medical staff are in short supply. In many places, such as

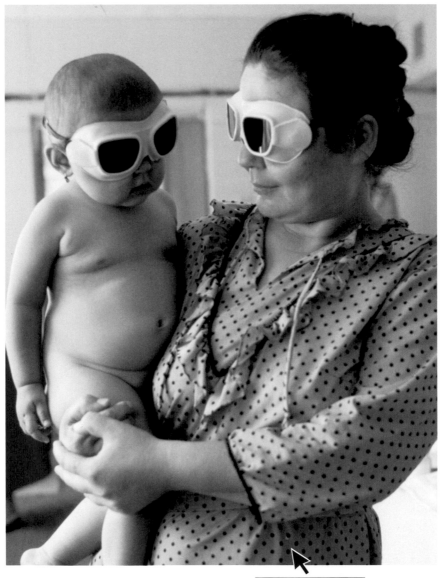

A child undergoes medical treatment at a research institute in Tashkent. Both the child and the caregiver wear dark glasses to protect their eyes during the treatment.

the Aral Sea region, drinking water is polluted. The polluted water leads to diseases such as typhoid, hepatitis, dysentery, cholera, and cancer. Air pollution causes additional ailments, such as asthma. Tuberculosis, a lung disease caused by bacteria, is another widespread health problem in Uzbekistan.

The infant mortality rate (the number of children who die under the age of 1) in Uzbekistan is 62 deaths per 1,000 births, almost ten times the rate recorded in the United States and other wealthy countries. The average life expectancy in Uzbekistan is 68 years for men and 73 years for women. These numbers are higher than those found in the world's poorest countries, but they are not as high as figures from the United States, Europe, and other wealthy places.

Many Uzbekistanis drink alcohol heavily. This habit often leads to additional health problems, such as liver and heart ailments. Drug addiction is another growing health problem in Uzbekistan. Heroin, an extremely dangerous drug, is readily available from nearby Afghanistan. Many young Uzbekistanis have become addicted to the drug. The United Nations Children's Fund (UNICEF) reports that illegal drug use in Uzbekistan increased fourfold between 1992 and 2002.

The human immunodeficiency virus (HIV) is not widespread in Uzbekistan. This virus causes AIDS, or acquired immunodeficiency syndrome. The virus most commonly spreads through sexual contact or intravenous drug use. Only 0.1 percent of the adult population is infected with the virus. But due to increased drug use in the early years of the twenty-first century, especially in big cities, the HIV rate in Uzbekistan is climbing quickly. Medical experts think that more than two thousand Uzbekistanis are infected with HIV. More than five hundred Uzbekistanis have died from AIDS. To combat AIDS, the government and private organizations have begun programs to teach people about HIV prevention.

Visit www.vgsbooks.com for links to websites with additional information about Uzbekistan's various ethnic groups, education, health care, and more.

◉ Woman's Rights

In traditional Uzbekistani society, the man was the head of the household. Women were expected to obey their husbands. Women did housework and farmwork and cared for children. They did not work outside the home. During the Soviet years, women achieved more equality in Uzbekistani society. Under the Soviet system, all citizens—male and female—attended school and held jobs.

Even after the breakup of the Soviet Union, women in Uzbekistan still work alongside men, and girls attend school in about the same numbers as boys. More than 60 percent of Uzbekistani women work outside the home. In 2004 seven women were members of the Uzbekistani legislature.

But many age-old attitudes about gender roles have not changed in Uzbekistan. Even though many women hold jobs, they earn less than their male coworkers and generally work in low-level positions. At home women are still expected to obey their husbands. In many homes, husbands batter their wives. The police rarely punish men for such abuse.

After independence, some women in Uzbekistan organized woman's rights groups. In addition to fighting for women's equality, these groups criticized the Karimov government for its censorship, repression, and human rights abuses. In response, the government passed laws that caused difficulties for woman's rights groups. Only government-approved groups were allowed to operate, and the government took control of funds coming to the groups from foreign countries. As a result, the woman's rights movement in Uzbekistan has stalled out.

WHITE BEARDS

Aksakals (meaning "white beards") are the elder men of the Uzbekistani community. Younger people treat them with great respect. Aksakals usually wear long beards, striped coats, and turbans on their heads *(below)*.

◉ Children in Uzbekistan

Uzbekistan has a young population. About 36 percent of its people are under the age of sixteen. Children's lives may be comfortable or miserable, depending on their family circumstances. Those children whose parents earn good salaries attend grade school,

A boy plucks cotton from a field. Many farm children in Uzbekistan hold part-time or full-time jobs.

high school, and perhaps college. But children from poor families often have to work instead. Their jobs range from street vending to construction to prostitution (sex work). Many children in rural areas help their families produce cotton, silk, and other crops. Some farm children attend school for only part of the year or not at all. The U.S. Department of Labor estimates that more than 23 percent of Uzbekistani children ages five to fifteen hold some kind of job.

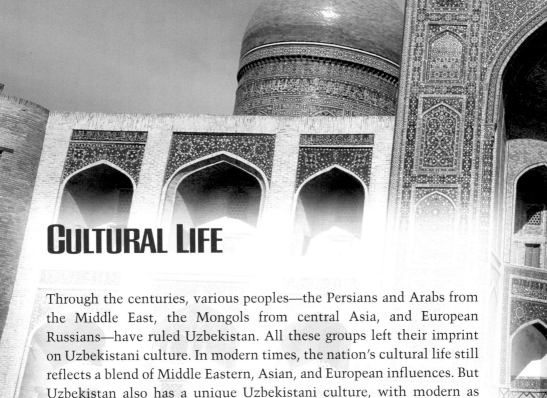

Cultural Life

Through the centuries, various peoples—the Persians and Arabs from the Middle East, the Mongols from central Asia, and European Russians—have ruled Uzbekistan. All these groups left their imprint on Uzbekistani culture. In modern times, the nation's cultural life still reflects a blend of Middle Eastern, Asian, and European influences. But Uzbekistan also has a unique Uzbekistani culture, with modern as well as ancient influences.

Language

Uzbekistan's official language is Uzbek. It is part of the Turkic family of languages. In ancient times, scholars wrote Turkic languages using the Sogdian alphabet. After Arabs conquered central Asia, people began to use a variation on the Arabic alphabet to write Uzbek and other Turkic languages.

In 1924 Soviet leaders decreed that people in central Asia would use the Latin alphabet (the alphabet used to write English and other

European languages) instead of Arabic. In 1940 the Soviets changed the alphabet again, this time to Cyrillic, the alphabet used to write Russian. By switching to Cyrillic, Soviet leaders hoped to further Russify the people of central Asia. The Soviets also made Russian the official language of Uzbekistan.

In 1994, after independence, the Uzbekistani government switched its alphabet back to Latin script and made Uzbek the nation's only official language. Many people in Uzbekistan still use Russian at work and in school. However, in an effort to reclaim their native tongue, Uzbekistanis have placed new emphasis on Uzbek language and literature. More and more, Uzbek has replaced Russian in government documents, textbooks, and street signs.

Some people in Uzbekistan also speak Tajik, the language of nearby Tajikistan. Some Muslim Uzbekistanis study Arabic, the language of the Middle East and the Islamic religion. Many young Uzbekistanis study English, the language of international business.

◉ Literature

Uzbekistan and the other central Asian nations have a long history of oral (spoken and not written) literature. In earlier centuries, traveling minstrels went from town to town and entertained audiences with songs, tales, and long poems called epics. One epic, *Alpamish*, tells detailed stories of good leaders engaged in fierce battles with evil ones. Considered Uzbekistan's national epic, the poem dates to the tenth century A.D. In addition to oral literature, many Uzbekistani writers recorded their words on paper. Poets, novelists, and scholars flourished in early Uzbekistan. One of the most famous was Ibn Sina (also known as Avicenna), an eleventh-century physician, philosopher, and writer.

Uzbekistan had a thriving literary community into the twentieth century. But during the Soviet era, the government strictly controlled and censored literature. Writers could produce only works that praised the Communist system. Soviet leader Joseph Stalin, who ruled as a dictator from 1929 to 1953, viewed writers and intellectuals as enemies of the people. Stalin had many Uzbekistani writers killed during his years in power.

Under the Karimov regime, Uzbekistani writers are not much better off. Government censors keep a strict watch over literary works. Any writer who criticizes the government risks harsh punishment. One group of writers, calling themselves the Fergana School, published a literary magazine in the early 1990s. But the government shut down the publication in 1994. Since independence, many writers have left Uzbekistan for nations that allow more freedom of expression.

◉ Architecture and Art

The architecture of Uzbekistan is closely linked to the Islamic religion. The nation's big cities, especially Samarqand, are filled with fine mosques, many dating to the fifteenth or sixteenth century. Most mosques have beautiful blue domes, grand arched entryways, and soaring minarets. Madrassas and mausoleums (aboveground tombs) are other impressive buildings seen frequently in Uzbekistani towns. Inside and out, the buildings are covered by colorful tiles—often blue or green—many decorated with intricate geometric patterns, floral images, or Arabic lettering.

Uzbekistan is also known for its beautiful folk art, with patterns and styles reflecting Asian, Middle Eastern, and Russian influences. This artwork includes useful household items such as woven wool blankets and hand-tooled leather bags. *Suzani* are richly decorated silk cloths used as wall hangings, bedspreads, and table covers. Uzbekistani jewelry incorporates semiprecious stones such as beautiful blue lapis lazuli. The town of Bukhara is famous for beautiful hand-dyed rugs. Intricate metalwork, wood carving, and calligraphy (stylized writing) are also part of the Uzbekistani folk art tradition.

The Telyashayakh Mosque in Tashkent is home to the oldest Quran (the Islamic holy book) in the world. The Othman Quran had belonged to Caliph Othman, the third successor to Muhammad (the founder of Islam). The Quran dates to the seventh century A.D.

During Soviet rule, the government required artists to make works that glorified the Communist system. Many paintings and sculptures depicted rugged farmers and factory workers, toiling tirelessly to create a better Soviet Union—a style called socialist realism. The Uzbekistani government still encourages artwork that glorifies the state. But it does not require artists to make specific kinds of images, and it does not monitor artists as strictly as it monitors writers. Many modern-day Uzbekistani artists make new works in traditional styles. Others create more contemporary paintings, ceramics, and sculpture.

A craftsman beats designs into copper. Uzbekistan has a rich folk art tradition, and many artisans continue to work in traditional styles.

Music and Dance

Uzbekistani music covers a wide range of styles. Many tunes reflect a Middle Eastern or Turkish influence, with fast rhythms and swirling melodies. Some Uzbekistani musicians perform simple folk songs, with little or no instrumental accompaniment. Other musicians perform in large groups.

Singing and music are common at Uzbekistani weddings, festivals, and other special occasions. Uzbekistani musicians play stringed instruments resembling lutes and guitars, wind instruments such as flutes, and percussion instruments such as drums, bells, and tambourines. The *dutar*, a two-stringed guitar, is particularly popular in Uzbekistan.

In earlier centuries, Uzbekistani folk musicians passed on their songs and tunes in person, without written notation. But one Uzbekistani musical style was written down. Called *maqam*, this kind of music began during Timur's reign. It was played in the

courts of local rulers and written according to strict rules. Composers of maqam divided their works into suites, or sections, each containing a certain kind of instrumental or vocal passage.

In modern Uzbekistan, young people like pop, rap, rock, and other modern musical styles. But unlike many singers in the United States, Uzbekistani performers make sure not to criticize the government with their song lyrics. Despite problems such as poverty and government repression, modern Uzbekistani musicians often sing of their nation's greatness. A woman named Yulduz Usmanova is the most famous Uzbekistani pop singer.

Dance has ancient roots in Uzbekistan, dating to the earliest human settlement there. Over the centuries, people in Uzbekistan developed different dances for different occasions, such as weddings, funerals, and festivals. Some dances focus on a single dancer. Others are group dances, performed in a circle. Most Uzbekistani dances involve intricate body movements. Dancers turn their wrists in circles, move their hands and arms in unusual patterns, twist and turn their bodies, and even dance on their knees. In some dances, performers make exaggerated facial movements or imitate the behavior of birds, fish, and other animals.

Women wearing traditional Uzbekistani clothing **perform a group dance,** while musicians play traditional instruments.

Modern Media

The Uzbekistani constitution guarantees freedom of the press. But in reality, there is almost no press freedom. The government owns many newspapers, radio stations, and TV stations. *People's Word* is a leading government-owned and government-operated newspaper with Uzbek- and Russian-language editions. The Uzbek State Television and Radio Company dominates the radio and television airwaves. Government-owned media always puts a progovernment spin on the news.

A variety of independent newspapers, TV stations, and radio stations also operate in Uzbekistan, but the government strictly monitors and censors these outlets. Any journalist who dares to criticize the government risks harassment and arrest. Some Uzbekistanis have cable and satellite TV, giving them access to foreign stations such as the British Broadcasting Corporation (BBC). However, the government sometimes blocks foreign news broadcasts.

Internet use is on the rise in Uzbekistan. In 2005 the nation had about 675,000 Internet users. Internet cafés are common in big cities. The government blocks some controversial Internet sites, but generally the Internet gives Uzbekistanis news and information they cannot get otherwise.

Uzbekistan has a small film industry. But because the government censors film along with all other media, Uzbekistani filmmakers shy away from controversial topics. Filmmakers generally make fictional films rather than documentaries.

Religion

In ancient times and in the early centuries A.D., the people of central Asia practiced many different religions. These religions included Buddhism and Zoroastrianism, an ancient Persian faith. In the eighth century A.D., Arab conquerors converted most central Asians to the Islamic religion. Even after the Arabs lost control of central Asia, Islam continued to thrive there. Timur and other leaders filled the cities of central Asia with thousands of spectacular mosques and madrassas.

In the nineteenth century, the Russians took over central Asia. At first, Russian conquerors let central Asians worship as they pleased. But

ISLAM IN CENTRAL ASIA

Islam has two main branches, Sunni and Shiite. Most central Asians belong to the Sunni branch of Islam. Some central Asian worshipers, called Sufis, practice a mystical form of Sunni Islam. Many central Asians also infuse Islamic worship with practices from Zoroastrianism and other pre-Islamic religions.

While facing southwestward, **Muslim men pray** at a mosque in Tashkent. Praying toward Mecca is the second pillar of Islam.

the situation changed with the creation of the Soviet Union. Soviet leaders despised religion and attempted to discourage and destroy it throughout their nation. They outlawed many Islamic practices, shut down madrassas and mosques, and arrested and killed Islamic leaders. By the 1980s, only a few hundred mosques were still open in all of central Asia. Despite government restrictions, some central Asians (and other Soviet citizens) practiced their faith in secret.

With independence, Uzbekistanis were once again free to worship openly. New mosques and madrassas sprung up throughout Uzbekistan. Some Uzbekistanis were only slightly religious. They followed some Islamic rules but not others. Other Uzbekistanis were extremely religious. They strictly followed the rules put forth in the Quran.

In the mid-1990s, several radical Islamic groups declared war on President Karimov's regime. These groups wanted Uzbekistani society

FIVE PILLARS OF ISLAM

Devout Muslims express their faith through five practices, called the Five Pillars of Islam. These pillars are:

1. Believing there is only one God, Allah, and that Muhammad was his prophet
2. Praying in the direction of Mecca (a holy city in Saudi Arabia) five times a day
3. Fasting from dawn to dusk during the holy month of Ramadan
4. Making a pilgrimage to Mecca at least once in a lifetime, if possible
5. Giving charity to the poor

to operate according to Islamic law. As part of the attack on Karimov, Islamic terrorists shot at government officials and bombed government buildings. In response, President Karimov cracked down on Islamic worship. Government agents harassed and arrested Islamic leaders and other devout Muslims. Many Muslims became afraid to worship openly.

In 2005, 88 percent of Uzbekistanis are Muslims—although most of them are not devout. About 9 percent of Uzbekistanis belong to the Eastern Orthodox Church, the main Christian church of Russia. The remaining 3 percent practice other religions, including Buddhism, Roman Catholicism, and Lutheranism. A small number of Jews live in Uzbekistan, mostly in the town of Bukhara.

Food

Uzbekistanis enjoy a variety of foods. Some favorite dishes have Middle Eastern origins. Others come from Russia, and still others are uniquely central Asian. Most big towns have a farmers' market, where cooks can buy fresh ingredients. People can buy cooked foods at street stalls, cafés, and restaurants.

An Uzbekistani family enjoys a meal at an open-air restaurant in Bukhara.

SABZI PIEZ

This tasty vegetable dish is a central Asian favorite.

3 tablespoons butter

1 medium-sized onion, thinly sliced and separated into rings

1 large tomato, peeled, seeded, and finely chopped

8 small carrots, sliced lengthwise into ⅛-inch-thick strips

½ teaspoon salt

⅛ teaspoon cayenne pepper

¼ cup finely chopped scallions

2 tablespoons finely chopped fresh cilantro

1. Melt butter in a heavy skillet over high heat.
2. Add onion rings to melted butter. Stirring frequently, cook over medium heat for 8 to 10 minutes, or until onion rings are golden brown.
3. Add tomato and increase heat slightly. Cook uncovered until most liquid in the pan has dried up.
4. Stir in carrots, salt, and cayenne pepper.
5. Add ½ to ¾ cup water (enough to just cover carrots). Bring to a boil, and cover skillet tightly.
6. Reduce heat to low, and simmer for about 10 minutes, or until carrots are tender.
7. Transfer contents to a serving bowl, sprinkle with chopped scallions and cilantro, and serve.

Serves 4 to 6

Grilled meat is a major ingredient in Uzbekistani cooking. Mutton, or sheep's meat, is most common, but people eat beef, chicken, and goat meat too. Shashlik is a dish made of meat and vegetables roasted on skewers. *Plov* is a dish of rice with meat, onions, carrots, and sometimes fruit. *Laghman* are heavy noodles, often served in a soup of mutton, peppers, tomatoes, and onions. Uzbekistanis eat a variety of dumplings—made from meat wrapped in dough and then boiled, baked, or fried.

Uzbekistanis eat lots of salads, made with tomatoes, cucumbers, carrots, cabbage, and other vegetables. Potatoes, pumpkins, and beans are also common in Uzbekistani cooking. Round, flat bread called *non* is served at every meal. Cooks liven up their dishes with cumin, red and black pepper, sesame seeds, dill, basil, and other herbs and spices.

Dairy products are abundant in Uzbekistani cooking. People drink milk from cows, sheep, goats, camels, and even horses. They also make milk into yogurt, cheese, and other foods. Ice cream is a popular dessert in Uzbekistan. Uzbekistanis also eat lots of apricots, raisins, figs, walnuts, peanuts, and almonds.

Holidays and Festivals

Uzbekistanis observe both religious and secular (nonreligious) holidays. Uzbekistan's Muslims observe the holy month of Ramadan, the ninth month of the Islamic calendar. During this month, Muslims take no food or drink from sunup to sundown. Evenings are devoted to prayer. At the end of the month, people hold a big feast called Eid al-Fitr. Members of the Eastern Orthodox Church observe Christian holidays such as Easter and Christmas.

Nonreligious holidays include New Year's Day (January 1), which Uzbekistanis celebrate with poetry, songs, and bonfires. People celebrate Navrus, an ancient spring festival (March 21), with street fairs, music, and large meals. Other secular holidays are International

Uzbekistani children admire a tree decorated for the new year in Samarqand.

Women's Day (March 8), Victory Day (May 9; commemorating the defeat of Germany in World War II), Independence Day (September 1), and Constitution Day (December 8).

 For more information about Uzbekistani culture, including crafts, sports, food, holidays, and more, visit www.vgsbooks.com for links.

Sports and Recreation

Many Uzbekistanis are accomplished athletes, especially in individual sports. Many Uzbekistani boxers and wrestlers have picked up gold and silver medals at the Olympic Games. Kurash is a martial (fighting) art that originated in central Asia more than 3,500 years ago. In this sport, two opponents wrestle each other in an upright, standing position. In the twentieth century, Kurash spread from central Asia to many other countries. Uzbekistan is home to some of the world's leading Kurash fighters. Uzbekistanis also enjoy team sports, especially soccer.

Horseback riding has been popular in Uzbekistan for centuries. *Buzkashi* is a rough game resembling rugby on horseback. But instead of using a ball, two teams of riders compete to carry the body of a dead sheep downfield and around a goalpost. The game is said to date to the days of Genghis Khan and his fierce horsemen. Horse racing is popular in Uzbekistan too.

Uzbekistanis like to spend their free time like people everywhere—visiting with friends and family, listening to music, and going to the movies. Uzbekistani men often gather at teahouses to eat, drink tea, and socialize. Chess is a popular pastime in city parks and teahouses. The nation's big cities are home to nightclubs and theaters, including the grand Alisher Navoi Opera and Ballet Theatre in Tashkent.

Uzbekistanis are big tea drinkers. Tea is called *choy* in Uzbekistan. Teahouses are called *choyhona*.

THE ECONOMY

Traditionally, most of Uzbekistan's people depended on farming to make a living. In the twentieth century, the economy expanded to include manufacturing, mining, and energy production.

Under Soviet rule, the central government in Moscow controlled the economy in Uzbekistan and every other Soviet republic. The state owned all farms and businesses. It controlled the production, marketing, sale, pricing, and transportation of goods and services.

After independence, the Uzbekistani government continued many of the economic policies of the Soviet Union. The government allowed people to open small businesses, but it kept tight control over large industries, agriculture, banking, and the flow of goods and services into, out of, and within the nation. This tight economic control discouraged foreign companies from investing and opening businesses in Uzbekistan.

Before independence, Uzbekistan was one of the poorest Soviet republics. In the years after independence, Uzbekistan remains very poor. Experts believe that 20 percent of the workforce is underemployed, or not working at regular, full-time jobs. More than three-quarters of the people live in poverty. Inflation, or rising prices, has made it difficult for Uzbekistanis to afford basic food and household goods.

⊙ Agriculture

Agriculture has long been the backbone of Uzbekistan's economy. In the early years of the twenty-first century, approximately 44 percent of Uzbekistanis make their living by farming. Farming accounts for 38 percent of the nation's gross domestic product (GDP), the total value of goods and services produced in the country in one year. Most farms in Uzbekistan are state owned.

Uzbekistan is one of the world's largest cotton producers. Most cotton farming takes place in the northwest, the east, and along the Amu River valley. Uzbekistan is also a leader in the cultivation of kenaf, a tough plant used to make rope, sacks, and paper. Farmers plant kenaf primarily in the Tashkent area. Farmers grow rice in the east and northwest of Uzbekistan. Wheat and barley production thrive near Samarqand and in the Kashkadarya region. Tobacco fields dot the eastern foothills and mountains. Silk production takes place in the Fergana Valley.

The fertile valleys of Fergana, Zeravshan, and Chirchik support orchards of apricot, cherry, fig, peach, and pomegranate trees. The vineyards of the Fergana and Tashkent regions produce grapes, which are made into wine or raisins. Samarqand and Tashkent are famous for vegetables, melons, and gourds.

Many Uzbekistani farmers raise livestock. The country is a leader in the breeding of Karakul sheep, famous for their high-quality wool. Chicken farms are common throughout the country. In the foothills and mountainous areas of Uzbekistan, farmers raise cattle and goats, which supply both meat

AN ANCIENT ART

Silk making is an ancient process that originated in China. The process begins with caterpillars called silkworms. Silkworms spin cocoons, or outer wrappings, around their bodies before turning into moths. The cocoons are made of silk. Silk farmers raise hundreds of silkworms on special farms. The farmers remove the worms' silk cocoons and process them into silk fabric. Uzbekistan is one of the world's leading silk producers.

A **silk factory** worker hangs raw silk on a rack. The silk will later be processed into fabric.

Uzbekistanis raise **Karakul sheep** for their wool. After sheep are sheared, their wool is spun into yarn or woven into fiber to make clothing.

and dairy products. In the western regions of the country, farmers breed horses and camels. People in Karakalpakstan raise muskrats, mink, and silver foxes for their valuable furs.

◉ Services

The service sector—which includes jobs in banking, tourism, communications, technology, education, and health care—is growing in Uzbekistan. The service sector accounts for 36 percent of Uzbekistan's GDP and employs 36 percent of the nation's workers.

Uzbekistan's service sector grew significantly in the early twenty-first century, because many Uzbekistanis opened stores, restaurants, taxi companies, and computer-related businesses. But opening a new service business in Uzbekistan is not easy. The government sets strict rules about business operations. These rules have discouraged some Uzbekistanis from running their own enterprises.

Uzbekistan has some impressive tourist destinations, such as the magnificent Silk Road cities of Bukhara and Samarqand. But because of government rules and regulations, it's hard for foreigners to get visas and other documents that allow them to visit Uzbekistan. Even so, the

Uzbekistani tourism industry is growing. Some Uzbekistanis have opened hotels, tour agencies, and other businesses that cater to tourists.

Manufacturing

Manufacturing accounts for 26 percent of Uzbekistan's GDP. About 20 percent of Uzbekistan's workers are employed in the manufacturing sector. The government owns or tightly regulates all big manufacturing businesses in the country.

Much manufacturing in Uzbekistan is closely tied to the country's farming sector. For example, some manufacturing plants turn local cotton and wool into clothing and shoes. Other plants build machines that farmers use to grow, harvest, transport, and process cotton. Some factories make farm fertilizers. Others produce cigarettes from tobacco, can fruit, process fish, or make wine.

Because it is such an important crop, cotton is nicknamed white gold in Uzbekistan.

Uzbekistan has nonagricultural manufacturing too. Some factories use local stone to make cement, concrete, bricks, and shingles. Other factories process metals or produce chemicals. In 1996 Daewoo, a South Korean car company, joined with an Uzbekistani firm to open an auto assembly plant in Andizhan. The plant employs several thousand Uzbekistani workers.

Mining and Energy

Uzbekistan is rich in metals. Workers mine gold in the Kyzyl Kum Desert and the Fergana Valley. Deposits of copper, zinc, lead, tungsten, and molybdenum come from the Olmaliq region, southeast of Tashkent. Uranium comes from mines on the edges of the Fergana Valley. Nonmetals, such as fluorite, sulfur, limestone, and marble, are also plentiful in Uzbekistan. Semiprecious stones and gems—such as turquoise, onyx, and garnet—are found in many areas of the country.

Natural gas is Uzbekistan's major energy resource. The largest gas deposits are in the Bukhara region. Coal mines lie near Tashkent and in the southern Surkhandarya region. Workers extract and process crude oil (petroleum) in the Fergana Valley, in the Bukhara region, and in southern areas of the country.

Because Uzbekistan has so much gas, coal, and oil, it can take care of its own energy needs and does not need to import fuel from other countries. In fact, Uzbekistan exports gas and other fuels to its central

Asian neighbors, as well as to Russia and other nearby countries. Many countries, have started to buy energy from Uzbekistan.

Transportation

Uzbekistan has a total of 50,700 miles (81,600 km) of roads. More than 87 percent of these roads are paved, but the roads are in poor condition, with many ruts and potholes. Railroads, carrying both freight and passengers, run between Uzbekistan's big cities. Private buses and shuttles, as well as personal cars, also carry people from city to city. In the city, people travel by taxi, bus, and car. Tashkent has a metro, or subway, system, but other Uzbekistani cities do not.

Passengers exit a train at a subway station in Tashkent.

> To learn more about Uzbekistan's economy, visit www.vgsbooks.com, where you'll find links to websites featuring information about farming, a currency converter, and more.

Tashkent International Airport is the major airline hub in central Asia. From there, passengers can take flights to big cities in Russia, Germany, Turkey, Pakistan, Iran, and other foreign nations. Samarqand also has an international airport. Smaller airports are found throughout the country. Uzbekistani Airways is the nation's major airline.

LAW AND DISORDER

Law and order is in short supply in Uzbekistan. The Russian Mafia—organized crime—operates in all the former Soviet republics, including Uzbekistan. The Mafia deals in illegal businesses such as drug sales, weapons trafficking, and prostitution. Members routinely bribe government officials to look the other way when they commit crimes.

The Uzbekistani government is known to be extremely corrupt—with officials eagerly taking bribes from criminals. Officials also demand bribes from honest people who want business licenses, admission to college, and other government services. Uzbekistani police officers also routinely take bribes.

◉ The Future

Uzbekistan sits at an important crossroads—geographically, economically, and politically. The nation occupies a strategic location between Asia, Europe, and the Middle East. Many larger nations want to take advantage of this location. For instance, the United States hopes to keep Uzbekistan as a long-term partner in its fight against Islamic extremists in the Middle East. But the United States also worries that Islamic extremism might grow stronger within Uzbekistan.

Russia and China are also keeping a close eye on Uzbekistan. These nations are wary about a strong U.S. presence in central Asia. Both nations have made military and economic agreements with Uzbekistan, hoping to strengthen their influence and power in the region. And because Uzbekistan is rich in coal, gas, oil, and other resources, many foreign countries see it as a valuable trading partner.

Among Uzbekistanis, many different forces are at work. The

government wants to maintain tight control over religion, the economy, and the media. Ordinary people want freedom, jobs, and the right to form political parties. Islamic Uzbekistanis want the right to worship freely, while the most extreme among them want to set up an Islamic government in Uzbekistan. Some Uzbekistani exiles—people who have fled the country to find safety and freedom elsewhere—are working from foreign countries to bring democratic changes to Uzbekistan.

Whose wishes will prevail? Will Uzbekistan's people ever know democracy, freedom of the press, freedom of speech, and freedom of religion? Only time will tell.

CA. 3000 B.C. Indo-Iranian nomads migrate through central Asia.

CA. 2000 B.C. Some central Asians settle into permanent farms and villages.

500s B.C. Cyrus the Great expands the Persian Empire into central Asia.

334–323 B.C. Alexander the Great conquers the Persian Empire.

323 B.C. Seleucus, one of Alexander's generals, takes control of central Asia and nearby lands.

100s B.C. Trade begins along the Silk Road, an overland route between China and Europe.

CA. A.D. 50 The Kushan come to power in central Asia.

500s Turkish conquerors take control in central Asia.

700s Arab armies conquer central Asia.

1200s Mongol warriors, led by Genghis Khan, invade central Asia.

1370 Timur takes control in central Asia. He oversees the creation of great mosques and artworks in Samarqand.

LATE 1400s The Uzbeks come to power in central Asia.

1500s Traders abandon the Silk Road in favor of sea routes between Asia and Europe.

1700s The Uzbek Empire breaks into small states called khanates.

1850s–1870s Russia conquers central Asia.

1914 World War I breaks out. Russia forces central Asians to provide food, supplies, and laborers for the war effort.

1917 Political activists called Bolsheviks lead a revolution in Russia. They set up a Communist government throughout all Russian-controlled lands.

1918 The University of Tashkent (later the National University of Uzbekistan) is founded.

1922 Russian-controlled territory is renamed the Union of Soviet Socialist Republics.

1924 Soviet leaders establish Uzbekistan as the Uzbek Soviet Socialist Republic, with Samarqand as its capital.

1929 Dictator Joseph Stalin comes to power in the Soviet Union. He begins a purge—or mass killing—of perceived enemies, including many Uzbekistanis.

1930	Tashkent becomes the capital of the Uzbek Soviet Socialist Republic.
1939	The Soviet Union enters World War II as an ally of Nazi Germany. Joseph Stalin relocates thousands of ethnic minorities to central Asia from other parts of the Soviet Union.
1941	Stalin joins forces with Britain and the United States against Nazi Germany
1940s AND 1950s	The Soviet government sets up heavy industries in Uzbekistan.
1960s	Soviet engineers build irrigation systems to divert river water to central Asian cotton fields. The Aral Sea begins to dry up.
1966	An earthquake hits Tashkent, destroying buildings and killing thousands of people.
1980s	Mikhail Gorbachev introduces glasnost, or openness, to the Soviet Union.
1991	The Soviet republics, including Uzbekistan, declare their independence. Uzbekistanis elect Islam Karimov as their first president.
1992	Uzbekistan joins the United Nations.
1994	Uzbek becomes Uzbekistan's official language.
MID-1990s	Radical Islamic groups launch terrorist attacks against the Karimov government.
1996	The Daewoo car company opens a manufacturing plant in Andizhan.
2000	Islam Karimov wins reelection as Uzbekistan's president.
2001	The United States declares war on the government in Afghanistan. Uzbekistan allows the United States to set up a military base in the town of Khanabad.
2005	Uzbekistani troops fire on demonstrators in Andizhan. The United States condemns the incident, leading to a breakdown in U.S.-Uzbekistani relations.
2006	The United States removes its soldiers from Uzbekistan.

COUNTRY NAME: Republic of Uzbekistan

AREA: 173,591 square miles (449,601 sq. km)

MAIN LANDFORMS: Kyzyl Kum Desert, Ustyurt Plateau, Zeravshan Valley, Chirchik Valley, Fergana Valley, Tian Mountains, Fan Mountains, Gissar Mountains

HIGHEST POINT: Beshtor Peak, 14,101 feet (4,298 m)

LOWEST POINT: Sariqarnish Kuli, 40 feet (12 m) below sea level

MAJOR RIVERS: Amu, Syr, Zeravshan

ANIMALS: antelope, bears, boars, camels, deer, falcons, hawks, lynx, mountain goats, pheasants, scorpions, sheep, snow leopards

CAPITAL CITY: Tashkent

OTHER MAJOR CITIES: Andizhan, Bukhara, Khiva, Samarqand

OFFICIAL LANGUAGE: Uzbek

MONETARY UNIT: Uzbekistani som. 1 som = 100 tiyins

UZBEKISTAN CURRENCY

Uzbekistan uses a unit of currency called a som. In Uzbek the word *som* means "pure" or "pure gold." The Uzbekistani government issues notes, or paper money, in denominations of 1, 5, 10, 25, 50, 100, 200, 500, and 1,000 soms. One som can be divided into 100 smaller units called *tiyins*. The government issues coins in denominations of 1, 5, 10, 25, and 50 tiyins. In 2006 it took 128 soms to equal one U.S. dollar.

Uzbekistan adopted its flag on November 18, 1991, shortly after declaring independence. The flag has three horizontal (sideways) bands. The top band is light blue, the middle band is white, and the bottom band is light green. Two thin red lines separate the three bands. The left side of the top band shows a white crescent moon and twelve white stars.

Each color and image on the flag carries a different meaning. The crescent moon symbolizes the rebirth of Uzbekistan as an independent nation. The twelve stars represent the twelve signs of the zodiac (or twelve months of the year). The blue band represents the sky and water. The white band stands for peace and purity. The green band represents nature and hope. The red lines stand for life.

Uzbekistan's national anthem is simply called "The National Anthem of the Republic of Uzbekistan." The tune comes from the old anthem of the Uzbek Soviet Socialist Republic, written in 1947 by composer Mutal Burhanov. After independence, in 1992, Abdulla Aripov wrote new lyrics for the anthem. Here are the words in English:

Stand tall, my free country, good fortune and salvation to you,
You yourself a companion to friends, Oh! Loving one!
Flourish, Oh! Creator of eternal knowledge and science,
May your fame for ever shine bright!

These valleys are golden—my dear Uzbekistan,
Our forefathers' manly spirits your companion!
Strength of great people in turbulent times
Made this land the world's joy!

Oh! Generous Uzbek, your faith will not fade,
Free, young generations are your mighty wings!
The torch of independence, guardians of peace,
Oh! Worthy motherland, flourish and prosper eternally!

 For a link where you can listen to Uzbekistan's national anthem, visit www.vgsbooks.com

LINA CHERYAZOVA (b. 1968) Lina Cheryazova is a champion in freestyle skiing, a sport in which athletes perform acrobatic stunts on skis. Born in Tashkent, Cheryazova became famous for performing the triple flip—somersaulting three times while soaring through the air on skis. She represented Uzbekistan at the Winter Olympic Games at Albertville, France, in 1992; in Lillehammer, Norway, in 1994; and in Nagano, Japan, in 1998. A defending world champion, she won a gold medal at the Lillehammer Games.

IBN SINA (980–1037) Also known as Avicenna, Ibn Sina was a famed medieval physician, philosopher, poet, and scientist. He was born in the small town of Afshana and educated in Bukhara. By the age of eighteen, he was practicing medicine. He traveled throughout Persia, working as a doctor for princes and other royalty. Ibn Sina wrote hundreds of manuscripts on religion, science, philosophy, medicine, and language. His most famous work is the fourteen-volume *Canon of Medicine*. For centuries, doctors in European countries used the work as a standard medical textbook. Another famous work, *The Cure*, involves Ibn Sina's interpretation of the philosophy of Aristotle.

ANTON JIVAEV (b. 1976) A native of Tashkent, Jivaev was born into a family of professional musicians. At the age of seven, he entered the Uspensky Special School of Music in Tashkent, where he studied violin. He furthered his musical education at the Tashkent State Conservatory and switched his specialty from violin to viola. He also learned to make and repair violas and violins. After graduation, Jivaev moved to the United States, where he studied at Duquesne University in Pittsburgh and the Curtis Institute of Music in Philadelphia. He has performed with the Pittsburgh Symphony Orchestra and other professional groups.

RUSTAM KASIMDZHANOV (b. 1979) Kasimdzhanov is an Uzbekistani chess champion. He holds the rank of grandmaster—the highest achievement in chess. Kasimdzhanov was born in Tashkent and began playing chess at the age of five. He excelled in junior tournaments, winning the World Junior Chess Championships in 1999. Kasimdzhanov had his greatest victory in 2004 when he won the World Chess Championships. In 2005 Kasimdzhanov was ranked number thirty-three in the world chess standings and number one in Uzbekistan.

MUHAMMAD SALIH (b. 1949) Muhammad Salih was born in Kharezm Province in western Uzbekistan. In college he began to write poetry. He published his first book of poems in 1977. In the late 1980s, Salih joined with other writers to form the Birlik (Unity) movement. The group worked for independence, democracy, and a better environment for Uzbekistan. A few years later, Salih left Birlik to form the Erk (Freedom) Party. In 1991 he became Erk's candidate in the election for the first president of Uzbekistan. But his opponent, Islam Karimov, used illegal tactics to win the election. Afterward, Karimov's government arrested many Erk members and shut down Erk newspapers. For his safety, Salih left Uzbekistan, moving to Turkey, Germany, Bulgaria, Switzerland, Russia, and Norway. From exile he continues to fight for democracy and freedom in Uzbekistan. He also continues to write poetry.

TIMUR (1336–1405) Timur, also known as Tamerlane, is revered in Uzbekistan as a great leader and conqueror. Timur was born near Samarqand. As a young man, he amassed more and more power until he finally controlled a powerful kingdom in central Asia. He made Samarqand his capital, where he oversaw the creation of grand mosques, elaborate artwork, and great literature. Starting in the 1370s, Timur's armies attacked neighboring territories, including Persia, India, and Egypt. His soldiers were brutal, often massacring thousands of civilians and enemy fighters alike. After Timur's death, his empire lost much of its power.

IRODA TULYAGANOVA (b. 1982) A native of Tashkent, Tulyaganova is a professional tennis player. She is a member of both the Women's Tennis Association (WTA) and the International Tennis Federation (ITF). She was a standout as a junior player, winning the Wimbledon junior title in 1999. She also turned pro in 1999. Although not a well-known player, Tulyaganova is a solid competitor, with seven WTA titles and seven ITF titles.

ULUGH BEG (1394–1449) Ulugh Beg was a prince, an astronomer, and a grandson of the great conqueror Timur. He was born in Soltaniyeh, a town in Iran, but he spent most of his life in Samarqand. Like his grandfather Timur, Ulugh Beg was a great lover of the arts. He was also passionate about history and astronomy. In the 1420s, he had a three-story observatory built in Samarqand. There, he studied the night sky. Through his observations, he discovered many errors in the calculations of Ptolemy, a famous second-century astronomer. When his father died in 1447, Ulugh Beg took over leadership of the Timurid Empire. Two years later, his enemies (including his own son) had him killed.

YULDUZ USMANOVA (b. 1963) Pop singer Yulduz Usmanova was born in the small Uzbekistani town of Namagan. As a young woman, she worked in a silk factory. She sang at weddings to earn extra money. In 1984 she enrolled at the Tashkent State Conservatory, where she honed her musical talents. Soon she was attracting large crowds at concerts and festivals in Uzbekistan and surrounding nations. Then she won fans worldwide. Usmanova has produced more than a dozen albums. Her music combines a pop sound with traditional Uzbekistani maqam music. Her band members also mix modern electric instruments with traditional Uzbekistani instruments.

APPLIED ARTS MUSEUM This museum in Tashkent displays the traditional arts of Uzbekistan: embroidery, wood carving, engraving, ceramics, and jewelry. Visitors will see many beautiful everyday objects, such as musical instruments, toys, pipes, and clothing. The building itself, created in 1898, is visually stunning as well.

BIBI-KHANYM MOSQUE This magnificent mosque in Samarqand dates to Timur's reign. An earthquake badly damaged the structure in 1897, but it has since been restored to its original splendor.

GURI AMIR MAUSOLEUM Timur, two of his sons, and two of his grandsons (including Ulugh Beg) are buried at this aboveground tomb in Samarqand. Construction dates to 1404. A giant block of dark green stone at the center of the tomb mark's Timur's grave. The mausoleum is topped by a stunning blue dome.

ICHON-QALA Ichon-Qala is the walled inner city of Khiva, home to a maze of restored madrassas, tombs, mosques, and palaces. As interesting as these structures are, the city walls themselves are even more fascinating. Made of mud and straw, they contain forty bastions (fortifications), as well as three gates.

LYABI-HAUZ This site in Bukhara is a plaza built around a pool. Shaded by mulberry trees, this is a peaceful spot where men play chess and sip tea. The plaza dates to 1620.

REGISTAN The Registan—a square plaza, surrounded by impressive buildings dating to medieval days—is the heart of Samarqand. Highlights include the Ulugh Beg Madrassa, dating to 1420; the Sher Dor Madrassa, finished in 1636; and the Tilla-Kari Madrassa, completed in 1660.

TOSH-KHOVLI PALACE This palace in Khiva holds splendid interior decorations, including ceramic tiles, wood carvings, and carved stone. Dating to the 1830s, the palace has more than 150 rooms, nine courtyards, and intricate soaring ceilings.

YODGORLIK SILK FACTORY At this factory in the town of Margilan, visitors can see the old-fashioned silk-making process, from unraveling silkworm cocoons to weaving fabric.

censor: to review information, such as news or literature, and to delete or change any objectionable content. In Uzbekistan the government censors writing and other creative works.

collective: a large farm that is owned and operated by the central government

Communism: a political system in which the government owns and controls all business, property, and economic activity

dictator: a leader who rules with absolute power

exile: a person who leaves his or her home country for a certain period. Sometimes exiles leave voluntarily, often to avoid government harassment. Other times, the government banishes exiles from the home country.

glasnost: a government policy, enacted in the Soviet Union in the 1980s, that gave people more freedom to discuss and write about political and social issues. The word *glasnost* means "openness" in Russian.

irrigation: a system of using pumps, channels, and other devices designed to carry water to crops

Mafia: an organized group that deals in illegal businesses

Muslim: a person who practices the Islamic faith

nomad: a person without a fixed home. Nomads move from place to place, usually to find new food supplies or to find food supplies for their animals.

Russify: a Soviet policy of making non-Russians use the Russian language, learn about Russian culture and history, and act more like Russians

Union of Soviet Socialist Republics: a nation that existed from 1922 to 1991; also called the Soviet Union or USSR. The Soviet Union had a Communist form of government. The Uzbek Soviet Socialist Republic was one of fifteen republics in the Soviet Union.

terrorism: the use of violence to create fear, usually for political purposes

Uzbek: a descendant of a tribal group that ruled central Asia in the fifteenth and sixteenth centuries

Selected Bibliography

Akbarzadeh, Shahram. *Uzbekistan and the United States: Authoritarianism, Islamism and Washington's New Security Agenda.* London: Zed Books, 2005.
After the September 11, 2001, terrorist attacks, the United States made an alliance with Uzbekistan. But the U.S.-Uzbekistani relationship is complex and fraught with difficulty. This scholarly work examines the intricacies of that relationship.

Allworth, Edward A. *The Modern Uzbeks: From the Fourteenth Century to the Present, a Cultural History.* Stanford, CA: Hoover Institution Press, 1990.
This scholarly work examines the Uzbek ethnic identity. The author discusses community, family, religion, culture, and other forces that unify the Uzbek people.

"Country Profile: Uzbekistan." *BBC News.* 2005.
http://news.bbc.co.uk/1/hi/world/asia-pacific/country_profiles/1238242.stm (May 2006).
This site provides an overview of Uzbekistani society, with links to in-depth articles on current events.

"Country Profile: Uzbekistan." *Library of Congress—Federal Research Division.* 2004.
http://lcweb2.loc.gov/frd/cs/profiles/Uzbekistan.pdf (March 2006).
This site offers extensive information on Uzbekistan's history, geography, society, economy, and government.

Glazebrook, Philip. *Journey to Khiva: A Writer's Search for Central Asia.* New York: Kodansha International, 1994.
The author details his travels through central Asia, with visits to the Uzbekistani cities of Khiva, Tashkent, Samarqand, and Bukhara. His travel narrative is interspersed with information on Uzbekistani history and culture.

Grousset, René. *The Empire of the Steppes: A History of Central Asia.* Translated by Naomi Walford. New Brunswick, NJ: Rutgers University Press, 1970.
Beginning with prehistory and ending with the Mongols, the author traces central Asian history in great detail.

Kleveman, Lutz. *The New Great Game: Blood and Oil in Central Asia.* New York: Grove Press, 2004.

Central Asia is rich in valuable oil and natural gas. Therefore, the United States, Russia, and China are all interested in control and influence in the region. This book examines the political complexities of this situation.

Mayhew, Bradley, Paul Clammer, and Michael Kohn. *Central Asia.* Footscray, Victoria, AUS: Lonely Planet Publications, 2004.
This well-researched guidebook is written for visitors to Uzbekistan, Kazakhstan, Kyrgyzstan, Tajikistan, Afghanistan, and Turkmenistan. The book offers comprehensive information on each nation's history, culture, and people, with practical details for travelers.

Moorhouse, Geoffrey. *On the Other Side: A Journey Through Soviet Central Asia.* **New York: Henry Holt and Company, 1990.**
The author traveled through central Asia in 1989, right before the demise of the Soviet Union. His book paints a vivid and complex picture of central Asian politics, culture, and society.

Olcott, Martha Brill. *Central Asia's Second Chance.* **Washington, DC: Carnegie Endowment for International Peace, 2005.**
After the fall of the Soviet Union, many people were hopeful that democracy would flourish in central Asia. So far, that hope hasn't been realized. The author investigates the reasons.

Rashid, Ahmed. *Jihad: The Rise of Militant Islam in Central Asia.* **New York: Penguin Books, 2003.**
Radical Islam is on the rise in the nations of central Asia, including Uzbekistan. The author examines the complexities of religion and politics in the region.

Roy, Olivier. *The New Central Asia: The Creation of Nations.* **New York: New York University Press, 2000.**
The author presents a thorough political analysis of the governments that have emerged in Kazakhstan, Turkmenistan, Uzbekistan, Tajikistan, Kyrgyzstan, and Azerbaijan since independence.

Thubron, Colin. *The Lost Heart of Asia.* **New York: Perennial, 1994.**
The author toured the five central Asian republics shortly after independence. His book offers insights into central Asian life and culture, with special emphasis on Uzbekistan.

"Uzbekistan," *CIA World Factbook.* **2005.**
http://www.cia.gov/cia/publications/factbook/geos/uz.html (March 2006).
Compiled by the Central Intelligence Agency, this site offers up-to-date facts and statistics on Uzbekistan's geography, environment, population, government, and economy.

"Uzbekistan Statistics," *UNICEF.* **2005.**
http://www.unicef.org/infoby country/Uzbekistan_statistics.html (March 2006).
This site, produced by the United Nations Children's Fund, offers statistics on nutrition, health, HIV/AIDS, education, economics, and other demographic areas.

Cheneviere, Alain. *Central Asia: The Sons of Tamburlaine.* **Paris: Vilo International, 2001.**
This lush photography book offers images of the people, land, and society of central Asia.

DK Publishing. *Islam.* **New York: DK Children, 2005.**
This beautifully illustrated book gives readers insight into Islam, the dominant religion in Uzbekistan.

Embassy of Uzbekistan to the United States
http://www.uzbekistan.org
This site offers a wealth of information about Uzbekistani news and society. Clicking on "About Uzbekistan" leads the visitor to good historical and cultural material.

Gottfried, Ted. *The Stalinist Empire.* **Minneapolis: Lerner Publications Company, 2002.**
Joseph Stalin imprisoned and murdered millions of Soviet citizens—including many Uzbekistanis—during his reign. This book sheds light on this brutal period in Soviet history.

Kalter, Johannes, and Margareta Pavaloi. *Uzbekistan: Heirs to the Silk Road.* **London: Thames and Hudson, 2003.**
Uzbekistan sat at the heart of the Silk Road and thus inherited artistic traditions from the East and the West. This book explores the gorgeous architecture, fine arts, and everyday crafts of Uzbekistan. Lush photographs illustrate the text.

Katz, Samuel M. *Jihad: Islamic Fundamentalist Terrorism.* **Minneapolis, Lerner Publications Company, 2003.**
This title explores major Islamic terrorist groups, such as al-Qaeda and Hezbollah, their history, their ideals, and important conflicts.

Khan, Aisha. *A Historical Atlas of Uzbekistan.* **New York: Rosen Publishing Group, 2003.**
Before it became an independent nation, Uzbekistan was part of many larger empires. This book uses a series of maps to explain the history of Uzbekistan from prehistoric to modern times. Text, photographs, and illustrations provide additional information.

Knowlton, Mary Lee. *Uzbekistan.* **New York: Benchmark Books, 2005.**
Part of the Cultures of the World series, this book introduces Uzbekistani history, culture, and government to young readers.

Kort, Michael G. *The Handbook of the Former Soviet Union.* **Minneapolis: Lerner Publications Company, 1997.**
This comprehensive reference book looks at the former Soviet republics, including Uzbekistan, and examines both their history and their futures.

Libal, Joyce. *Uzbekistan.* **Broomall, PA: Mason Crest Publishers, 2005.**
This book for young readers examines the growth of Islam in Uzbekistan and other Asian nations.

Further Reading and Websites

Ma, Yo-Yo. *Along the Silk Road*. Seattle: University of Washington Press, 2002.
Acclaimed cellist Yo-Yo Ma created this book to promote the music, art, and culture of the nations that sat along the old Silk Road. Essays and beautiful photographs shed insight into the history, culture, and people of Uzbekistan and other central Asian nations.

McCray, Thomas. *Uzbekistan*. New York: Chelsea House Publications, 2004.
This book provides a thorough introduction to Uzbekistan and the problems it faces in the twenty-first century.

Ross, Stewart. *The Collapse of Communism*. Chicago: Heinemann, 2004.
This book for young readers examines the Communist philosophy and how Communism ultimately failed in the Soviet Union.

Schneider, Mical. *Between the Dragon and the Eagle*. Minneapolis: Carolrhoda Books, 1996.
Discover the ancient Silk Road in this book that follows a bolt of silk hand-crafted in China along the Silk Road to the Roman Empire.

Spencer, William. *Islamic Fundamentalism in the Modern World*. Minneapolis: Twenty-First Century Books, 1997.
This title gives readers an overview of Islam and how Islamic fundamentalism has shaped the modern world.

Traditional Culture and Folklore of Central Asia.
http://intangiblenet.freenet.uz/eng.htm
Visitors to this site can click on links to the nations of central Asia and learn about their traditional architecture, music, folklore, and more.

UzDessert: Your Guide to Uzbek Culture.
http://www.uzdessert.uz
Visitors can learn about Uzbekistani food, history, music, art, film, literature, and dress at this fact-filled website.

vgsbooks.com
http://www.vgsbooks.com
Visit vgsbooks.com, the home page of the Visual Geography Series®. You can get linked to all sorts of useful online information, including geographical, historical, demographic, cultural, and economic websites. The vgsbooks.com site is a great resource for late-breaking news and statistics.

Yancey, Diane. *Tuberculosis*. Minneapolis: Twenty-First Century Books, 2001.
This title from the Twenty-First Century Medical Library examines the disease tuberculosis through case studies and information from experts.

Zuelke, Jeffrey. *Joseph Stalin*. Minneapolis: Lerner Publications Company, 2006.
The Stalin era was a particularly bleak one for Uzbekistan and the other central Asian nations. This insightful biography examines the cruel dictator who brought terror and despair to the Soviet Union.

Captions for photos appearing on cover and chapter openers:

Cover: A statue of a camel caravan in Samarqand

pp. 4–5 The Zeravshan Valley

pp. 8–9 Tour buses are parked in a line in front of Independence Square in Tashkent. Independence Square is the largest city square in the former Soviet Union.

pp. 36–37 A group of Uzbekistanis in Tashkent reflects a mix of old and new—some are dressed traditionally while others wear Western clothing.

pp. 46–47 The Mir-i-arab Madrassa (Islamic school), dating from the sixteenth century, stands in Bukhara. Mir-i-arab was central Asia's only operating madrassa during Soviet rule of the region.

pp. 58–59 Women sell produce at a bazaar in Andizhan. Many Uzbekistanis make their living by farming.

Photo Acknowledgments
The images in this book are used with the permission of: © Martin Barlow/Art Directors, pp. 4–5, 18; © XNR Productions, pp. 6, 11; © age fotostock/ SuperStock, pp. 8–9, 24 (bottom), 26; © 1996 CORBIS; Original image courtesy of NASA/CORBIS, p. 10; Library of Congress, pp. 13 (top; LC-DIG-prokc-21780), 28 (LC-USW33-024255-C), 29 (LC-USW33-024222-C); © Joe & Mary Ann McDonald/Visuals Unlimited, p. 13 (bottom); © Ken Lucas/Visuals Unlimited, p. 14; © Andrew Cunningham/Visuals Unlimited, p. 15; © Earl & Nazima Kowall/CORBIS, pp. 16–17; © North Wind Picture Archives, pp. 22, 24 (top); Mary Evans Picture Library/Meledin Collection, p. 27; © TENGKU BAHAR/ AFP/Getty Images, p. 31; © VIKTOR KOROTAYEW/Reuters/Corbis, p. 33; © Victor Kolpakov/Art Directors, pp. 36–37, 41, 63; © Robin Smith/Art Directors, pp. 39, 40, 45, 49; © Janet Wishnetsky/CORBIS, p. 42; © Tibor Bognar/ Art Directors, p. 44, 46–47; © Trip/Art Directors, pp. 50–51, 53; © Chris Rennie/ Art Directors, p. 54; © WAYMAN RICHARD/CORBIS SYGMA, p. 56; © Brian Vikander/Art Directors, pp. 58–59; © Wolfgang Kaehler/CORBIS, pp. 60–61; © Lynda Richardson/CORBIS, p. 61; Audrius Tomonis—www.banknotes.com, p. 68; Laura Westlund/Independent Picture Service, p. 69.

Front Cover: © Tibor Bognar/Art Directors. Back Cover: NASA